Yesterday's Tomorrow

Yesterday's Tomorrow

On the Loneliness of Communist Specters and the Reconstruction of the Future

Bini Adamczak

translated by Adrian Nathan West
foreword by Raymond Geuss

The MIT Press / Cambridge, Massachusetts / London, England

Originally published in 2007 as *Gestern Morgen: Über die Einsamkeit kommunistischer Gespenster und die Rekonstruktion der Zukunft* (c) edition assemblage & Unrast Verlag 2011.

Foreword by Raymond Geuss originally published in *Radical Philosophy* 186 (2014): 58–59, © Radical Philosophy Ltd.

This book was set in Arnhem Pro and Bebas Neue Pro by Westchester Publishing Services. Printed and bound in the United States of America.

Library of Congress Cataloging-in-Publication Data

Names: Adamczak, Bini, author.
Title: Yesterday's tomorrow : on the loneliness of communist specters and the reconstruction of the future / Bini Adamczak ; translated by Adrian Nathan West ; foreword by Raymond Geuss.
Other titles: Gestern Morgen. English
Description: Cambridge, Massachusetts : The MIT Press, 2021. | Originally published in German under title: Gestern Morgen. | Includes bibliographical references.
Identifiers: LCCN 2020021696 | ISBN 9780262045131 (hardcover)
Subjects: LCSH: Communism—History. | Communism—Soviet Union—History. | Soviet Union—History—1917-1936.
Classification: LCC HX40 .A48513 2021 | DDC 335.43—dc23
LC record available at https://lccn.loc.gov/2020021696

10 9 8 7 6 5 4 3 2 1

**WE WHO WANTED TO PREPARE THE GROUND
FOR FRIENDLINESS**

How much earth will we have to eat
With the taste of our victims' blood
On the way to the better future
Or to none, if we spit it out
—Heiner Müller, *Werke 1: Die Gedichte*

Contents

Foreword by Raymond Geuss / ix

1   **End** / 1
2   **Farewell** / 23
3   **Party** / 45
4   **Class** / 83
5   **Promise** / 103
6   **Revolution** / 123
7   **PS** / 155

Acknowledgments / 157
Notes / 159
Remembrance (Bibliography) / 165

Foreword

This is a book about "communist desire"—that is, about the deep-seated moving force within people that impels them to strive to give their lives self-chosen collective meaning by opposing oppression and arbitrary coercion, abolishing hierarchical structures, and ending the various forms of alienation. The attempts to act on this desire in the twentieth century were a series of colossal and catastrophic failures. What took place in the huge region of Eurasia that was once organized as the Russian Empire and then became the Soviet Union between 1917 and 1939 provides an instructive instance of the way in which utopian hopes, energies, and aspirations can turn against themselves, becoming more destructive the more well founded and disciplined they seemed to be. How, in the face of this, can it be at all reasonable even to try to keep any kind of grip on the utopian contents of communist desire?

Part of the answer, Bini Adamczak argues in this book, must lie in a reflection on the history of the failures of the communist project in the twentieth century. We can only reasonably hope to retain and cultivate a "communist" desire for a utopian future if we understand the nature of past utopian desires and the specific ways in which they failed. Each of a series of chapters in Adamczak's book is devoted to exploring one historically concrete situation in which this failure became manifest: the Hitler–Stalin Pact, the Great Terror of 1937–1939, the failure of the Left in Central Europe to stop the advent of National Socialism, Joseph Stalin's rise to power, and Kronstadt. Adamczak puts particular emphasis on the way in which agents in the past did or did not realize while it was happening that their commitments were turning against themselves, transforming them into their opposite, and becoming destructive. The failures, the author holds, are *real* failures, and although much can be said about how they are to be best understood, nothing is to be gained cognitively, morally, or politically by closing one's eyes to them, pretending they did not occur, or trivializing them. It is also essential to the future survival (or revival) of hopes for a better future that the work of understanding and mourning be completed in such a way as not to give succor to those who would systematically root out communist desire.

The order in which the failures are presented and discussed in Adamczak's book is the reverse of the historical order in which they occurred (the Hitler–Stalin Pact first; Kronstadt last). This is part of a conscious strategy of the author, who thinks that those who broadly share the ideals and aspirations of the major agents and victims in this story have a natural tendency to think of the history of this period in this way, looking back from the present and locating at some point in the past a moment of unmitigated "good" that however passed, was lost and then initiated a historical process of degeneration. The natural question to ask is, "Where and when did it go wrong—when Stalin signed the pact with Adolf Hitler, or *already* in 1933, or with Kronstadt?" Part of the point of the book, as I understand it, is to reject this as the right way to understand and come to terms with what happened. There was *never* a single moment in the past in which an aboriginally pure revolutionary will or unsullied communist desire was fully present and on the point of realizing itself, which then passed, was lost, and was perverted or corrupted. When you peel the layers of the historical onion back, you come not to a "pure" onion at the heart but to nothing. This does not mean that an onion is not an onion, or that "nothingness" is the core of the onion, but rather just that one must think about the onion in a different way.

Although the above description may give the impression that this is a book of "history," it is in fact a particularly admirable feature of the book that it does *not* fall into any of the usual categories. If I had to describe it, I would say it is a lyrical and philosophical reflection on history in the service of a rekindling of utopian desire. "Lyrical" is not a word that is automatically associated with sober analysis, realism, or scholarship. This work has *all* those virtues, but also a remarkable lightness of touch, and an unsentimental ability to enter into the mental and psychic worlds of those who are now dead and present their world (including the nonworld of their unfulfilled aspirations) in a way that retains its full human vitality. "Real history"—the story of what did happen—and the history of utopian desire—an account of what people at any given time thought ought to happen—are not only compatible but also require each other if we are to retain any hope for the future at all.

—Raymond Geuss

1 End

In every generation there must be those who live as if their time were not a beginning and an end, but rather an end and a beginning.
—Manès Sperber, *Wie eine Träne im Ozean*

The last warm rays of the sun expire. Not a single bird takes off from the leafless trees, not a single wing beat can be heard. As if they have forgotten the point of flying, have lost the faith in being borne up by the air, the creatures perch on the slender branches. Slowly the long shadows of the telegraph poles, once meant to connect a continent to come, retreat in the harvested fields. The odd forgotten blade of grass waits motionless in the windless early dusk, in the distance scattered woodlands mingle with border villages history has forgotten. It's getting dark.

Just maybe, though, there is a bit of light left. A fleeting night offers a glimpse of landscapes animated by unchanged field work. Here and there the dew clings to the waves of grain. The first cars take to the road, and for a few kilometers, they pass alongside the railway. Something warm seeps through the tiny cracks in the vehicle. At times the fog still clouds the view, which even without it would not be clear. After the daylong journey from Moscow, or further away, on to the Russian border, their eyes can grow weary watching the fields, which rush past and yet, in their immensity, seem stationary. But the eyes of the German antifascists, the communist emigrants, see nothing, there are no windows in their barred compartments. Perhaps outside, the first patches of light are grazing the ground while the mountains on the horizon stretch their stony heads upward into the dawning day.

Or maybe it's already daytime. Possibly, even probably, it is bright out, because the weather bends seldom to the history writer's metaphoric wishes. A radiant day, white from the snow on the summits in the distance, from the glittering of the wide rivers, the multitudinous Polish lakes. The almost noonday sun stands in the otherwise empty sky, warms the roofs of the Stolypinski carriages, rolling prisons where the inmates sit seven to a car. The rattling of the train makes conversation between one compartment and the other impossible. For a time songs are audible, and encouraging words, but then, all at once, they fall silent. The wardens bring water and generous helpings of food, but now the prisoners have lost their appetite. "Why now? Just eat! There's plenty of time for you to go hungry later!" one of the soldiers tells them kindly (Buber-Neumann, 182f.). The soldiers are from the NKVD, the People's Commissariat for Internal Affairs, and they have been ordered to bring a sealed cargo across the border—a silent, human cargo.

When the train slows down, the sun perhaps reaches its zenith, nature shows itself blind to history. In the train station, the antifascist prisoners step out, walk on foot for the final wooded stretch. On the train bridge from Brest-Litovsk, the newly established border, the road comes to an end. Other soldiers come from the other side of the bridge, raise their hands to their caps to greet the officers of the NKVD (ibid., 185f.). The names are read out, the exchange begins. Those who resist in panic are shoved, and the German soldiers—the SS soldiers—receive the Jews in their ranks with anti-Semitic tirades.

A train of many trains, of forgotten trains. Special trains in which the NKVD transport German or Austrian communists to the German border, deliver them to the Gestapo. First on different tracks, depending on their place of incarceration, through Shepetovka and Negoreloe/Stowbsty and on to the Polish border, through Būcmaņi in Latvia, through Ostrow, or through Finland (Schafranek, 40). Then, once Germany and Russia share a common border, exclusively through Brest-Litovsk, the same Brest-Litovsk where, two decades before, Leon Trotsky met with diplomats from the Central Powers to make peace, to salvage the revolution. Of the thousand deportees, embassy and secret service files document conclusively more than three hundred communists, Jews, and antifascists.[1] A multitude of transports, the first already in 1935, the last in May 1941, a month before the outbreak of the war (R. Müller, 9; Schafranek, 56). And only two are commemorated, in the publications of Margarete Buber-Neumann and Alexander Weissberg-Cybulski in spring 1940.

Most of those traveling in the trains from Russia to Germany are engineers, specialists, skilled workers whose contracts have expired and who have been released for the journey home. Some of the prisoners are National Socialist sympathizers, a number of them spies under orders from the German regime. Others, though—and these are the ones who concern us *for now*—are communists, mostly members of the German Communist Party or of the Austrian Schutzbund. They arrived in the Soviet Union as supporters of revolution, and most remained until 1933 or 1934. Some of them left only later, after years of fighting in the underground, building and rebuilding the Communist Party, the KPD, without cease until their cover was blown and they had to escape. Many of them have been in German prisons, have suffered torture, some in the first concentration camps. They are antifascists, they even have the state's seal of approval, and the Soviet authorities are strict in these matters. Only those who engaged in active resistance according to the standards of the KPD are allowed to immigrate; anti-Semitic persecution isn't enough to qualify for an offer of asylum.[2]

Persecuted by the Nazis, fleeing the threat of the camps, German and Austrian communists flee into Russian exile, into the Soviet Republic, the fatherland of the workers, of the proletariat, to Moscow, the reddest city on the planet. Protection is not what they hoped for most, but the chance to go on contributing to the construction of socialism, to organize resistance to Germany in exile. Very few of them mean to stay, they want to go back, with new papers, with a different mission. And back they go, but unarmed, not as revolutionaries, as Soviet soldiers, but rather as their captives.

They come from the labor camps, from Karaganda in Kazakhstan, from the penitentiaries of the Solovetsky Islands in the White Sea, or directly from the detention centers in Kharkiv, Gorki, or Engels, where they sit for years, awaiting trials that always proceed according to the same manner. They are shipped in from the most far-flung regions of the Soviet Republics, transported thousands of kilometers, individually or in small groups. Some are old acquaintances by now, as they find themselves once more in group cells in Butyrka, Moscow's central prison, where many were placed after their initial arrests a few years before. But now, unlike before, there are only 25 of them, not 110 lodged in a cell built for 25, and they sleep on beds, not on boards, on mattresses with sheets rather than on the floor wrapped in their coats. Instead of nodding off—nodding off, not sleeping!—they sit in chairs, and instead of whispering they talk loud and play games. Before, they were forbidden even to walk around, let alone sew or sing (Buber-Neumann, 34ff., 164ff.; Weissberg-Cybulski a, 333). They receive medicine, good food, not the watery soup from before, but generous meals served three times a day. Their hunger that plagued them during their years in remand, that spurred them to forced labor in the camps, is stilled on the eve of their extradition. As if the involuntary deportees should make a good impression on those who would receive them, in this way shining a pleasant light on their host country. Less, presumably, to persuade the Nazis of the humanity of the Soviet prison regime than to demonstrate the Red Empire's largesse, which is enough to spare wholesome provisions for its captives. The latter, naturally, see things otherwise: they have rather been fattened up for delivery to the German butcher (Buber-Neumann, 169 f.).

That's how it seems, but only a few speak of it, only a few dare to speak of what seems likely but at the same time impossible. Among them is Zenzl Mühsam—arrested not long after arriving in the Soviet Union to spread word of the Nazi's crimes, of the murder of Erich Mühsam. Unlike others, she realizes she may be extradited after the pact between Germany and Russia, and she refuses to sign her deportation order "abroad" without specifying a destination. Better to throw herself on the train tracks than go back to Germany, better to stay in the Stalinist prison network. And she does stay, in jails, in camps, and in exile before migrating to East Germany, the GDR, in 1955. Her warnings fall on deaf ears, no one shares her suspicions. Almost no one, irrespective of the privations, degradations, disfigurement suffered at the hands of the NKVD, considers—is willing to consider—deportation to the Germans possible. Even on the train, they are unwilling to accept it, they encourage one another, vow that after setting off toward Poland, despite all logistical reason, they would be turning back toward Minsk, veering off toward Lithuania (ibid., 181). They will not, cannot believe otherwise. How firm their faith must have been to go on disbelieving, after years of imprisonment and forced labor, in the crime about to occur.

As inconceivable, almost as inconceivable, as the deportations themselves, the expulsion of communists by communists, a gift to the Nazis from the hands of the Nazis' mortal enemies. So inconceivable that not even the Gestapo can believe it, and takes a large proportion of the antifascists, people who had often been jailed on the charge of *fascist espionage*, to be agents of the GPU, the Soviet Secret Service (Schafranek, 94f.). Even more so, because the Germans expressly oppose many of the deportees' repatriation and refuse to accept them numerous times, at least until 1939. The German Embassy and the Foreign Ministry want Germans, not anti-Germans, not *enemies of Germany* (ibid., 69). They want *Volksdeutsche*, the people with German roots, not Jews, the expatriates, antifascists. And yet they get them, to the Gestapo's great delight. Eighty antifascists before the 1939 Hitler–Stalin Pact, more than 200 (out of 350 deportees) afterward (ibid., 44, 48, 69, 79). Only now do the Germans press for deportations, stressing the *mutual friendly relations between the German Reich and the USSR* (Ambassador Friedrich-Werner Graf von der Schulenberg, cited in ibid., 184). There is no evidence of other pressure, nor of any "reciprocation" to follow. The Nazis give the numbers, the Soviets supply the names. The antifascists are sacrificed not according to some overarching principle of political calculus nor as currency in an exchange but rather as a kind of gift (cf. ibid., 56f.).

Though every detainee designated "repatriated from Russia" is "politically suspect" for the Gestapo, they conclude that the majority of those "infected with Marxism" have been "thoroughly healed of Bolshevik conditioning," and quite often they are correct (ibid., 89). Buber-Neumann describes how many of the detainees handed over and interned in German prisons lose their faith in the Soviet Union, grow convinced of a German victory, and predict a bright future for National Socialism. Some even find positive aspects in it, discovering socialist traits in the economy and the workers' legislation. Already in Moscow, Weissberg-Cybulski (b, 687) witnesses such discussions:

The prisoners in the deportees' cell in Butyrka stood ... with the weight of both systems bearing down on them. They still feared the GPU, and were now afraid of the Gestapo as well. Loose talk could still bring down the wrath of the Stalinist system. A few weeks later, excessive loyalty to the Soviets might provoke the same from the Gestapo. We had to be cautious, a GPU snitch might be sitting in our cell even then. Not to mention those who would snitch, those who had already decided to betray their fellow man to curry favor with the Germans. In these conditions, just opening your mouth was inadvisable.

Still in the deportation cell, there is a scuffle between Weissberg-Cybulski and a former collaborator of the Comintern for whom National Socialism is a form of organized capitalism that would pave the way for socialism.[3] An anti-Stalinist, but still socialist Jew against a no-longer-Stalinist, National Socialist German.

"I should have stayed quiet," writes Weissberg-Cybulski (ibid., 694). "Carrying on with this conversation was dangerous. ... The majority of the workers in the cell were smarter than I was. They chose the one correct path in this complicated situation: silence."

The workers—those unwilling to repeat what was dictated to them—say nothing. But this is not a shared silence, but a lonesome one, based on mistrust, on fear of one's neighbor. They say nothing because the things they say might be heard—not listened to, but *overheard*. They say nothing out of fear, but not only out of fear: it is also that they have no say, nothing to share, their fate will be discussed, their destiny decided, between one embassy and another, one state and another. It leaves them speechless—well, not "it," if there were indeed such an it, but rather the NKVD and Gestapo, whose enigmatic handshake implicated their very bodies.

And these are the ones who will also make them talk, in countless interrogations from bureaucratic to brutal: first the NKVD, and then the Gestapo in Poland or in Germany. The latter will divide them into groups according to the danger they represent, A, B, and C, and will send them off to German factories and barracks or penitentiaries or concentration camps. Many are sent to their place of origin, where they must register with the authorities and labor in German firms under close observation (Buber-Neumann, 197). Many—maybe most—are recruited into the Wehrmacht, and not seldom—here is yet another twist—do they return to the Soviet Union, as soldiers in the war of extermination waged against the Red Army.

Take, for example, the case of Erwin Jöris—though he is not an example, really, not a case, but instead quite singular—who is imprisoned as the leader of the Berlin-Lichtenberg Communist Youth League and remains incarcerated, with Erich Mühsam, among others, for a year in the Sonnenberg concentration camp. No sooner is he released than he joins the antifascist underground and remains there until 1935, when his organization is exposed and he is forced (and able) to flee, first to Prague and then on to Moscow. Only to be arrested in 1937 and sent back in 1938, this time to Poland and then on to Germany. After a year in remand in Moabit, he is freed by the Gestapo and recruited by the Wehrmacht. In 1944, he is taken war prisoner by the Soviets, omits mention of his first visit to the country, and moreover, speaks not a word of Russian for two long years, despite his thorough mastery of the language. After his release in 1946, he returns to Berlin and there runs into an old acquaintance by the name of Eric Honecker, whom he tells that he has lost all interest in politics. Two weeks later, the NKVD arrest him on the basis of declarations he made to the Gestapo concerning the Soviet Union, he is sentenced to twenty-five years of hard labor in Workuta (Scholmer, 98ff.).

Then there is Franz Langer—again, not just an example—who becomes an affiliate of a Schutzbund group (a Social Democratic paramilitary organization) in 1934, flees to Czechoslovakia after the battle against the Austrian fascists in Vienna-Ottakring, and there joins the Communist Party. In 1938, he is arrested and transported from Moscow to Germany in 1940; in June of that year, the Wehrmacht deploys him. In March 1945 he manages to desert and shows up in Vienna, where he will later establish contact with the Red Army and fight with it against the Nazis and their *Volkssturm* units (Schafranek, 146).

Lunatic twists, multiple twists, which take place—in utterly distinct yet not unrelated ways—in the opposite direction, in the lives of Soviet prisoners of war interned in German forced labor camps, who were arrested on release by the NKVD and again sentenced to forced labor, this time in Soviet camps (ibid., 107; Buber-Neumann, 347). They are caught between the gears, emigrants unable to immigrate, flung across the continents, ground up in the gears of the Great Powers, the teeth of which gnash like teeth in a mouth stretched into an inhuman rictus.

Not all the deported antifascists are freed after their interrogation to labor for the German cause or to fight as soldiers. The Gestapo's orders exclude those who "were active Marxist militants prior to emigration, who engaged in political activities in the Soviet Union, who agitated against Germany, or who continue to cling to their Communist convictions" as well as those "of Jewish lineage" (Schafranek, 180). For these people, "return" means to prisons and ghettos, to concentration and extermination camps. Only a few survive; the rest will die there. In Lublin, in Neuengamme and Mauthausen, in Auschwitz and Majdanek.

Like spokes in a wheel, which seem to stand still, then turn backward, once it reaches a certain speed, these trains travel back from Socialist Russia into National Socialist Germany. In the opposite direction of the sealed train that, decades before, had brought Lenin to Petrograd to wage revolution. Unceasing progress, which was meant to push history toward Communism, with an inevitable leap from the first revolution in 1917 to the second, then to the worldwide one, ends here. Not halfway—how nice that might have been—not at the beginning, but even earlier. In the camps, almost naturally those of the enemy, but also, incomprehensibly, those of one's allies. Double betrayal. Betrayal of antifascism, betrayal of communism—you rarely get the first without the second, and you never have the second without the first. But above all, betrayal of the communists, of one comrade by the other. Betrayed to those whom they had fought against for the better part of their lives from 1918 on, who were the focal point of their political rage, betrayed by those for whom they had devoted their lives, for whom they were willing to sacrifice their lives. Without a name, they die, without a struggle, most of them, not at the barricades, but behind them, in Moscow's prisons, deep in the Siberian steppes, back in the German camps. They counted on dying, on an early and violent death. But they do not die for revolution, nor for communism, if such a thing exists. For them, there will never be any communism. There is no communism for them. There is no communism without them. There will never be any communism without them.

But how are we to remember them? How do we remember those of whom there is so little left to remember? And above all, with whom do we remember them? To whom do we raise the alarm, whom do we warn or turn to for help? Who do we call to in the name of a justice deferred, past due, of zealous partisanship for those the party betrayed? With whom do we mourn the lost, the murdered, the abandoned revolutionaries? Abandoned in the train cars, hiding out in another country, betrayed in the concentration camps, subdued in tiny apartments in Moscow, in jail cells, in Siberian work camps. They have no allies left, no friends across the border, no fellow fighters, no comrades back home, no one who takes heart at the thought of them, no one they might think of to fire their hopes. With whom to share their loneliness? At least that. At least to offer them companionship, imaginary, belated companionship.

At the moment when they are awaiting arrest, for example, tipped off by the disappearance of some of their comrades, the ones who were critical first, as it may seem in the beginning. Tipped off, perhaps, by the great show trials, which they may no longer be so inclined to justify as do the major communist intellectuals elsewhere (Brecht, Feuchtwanger), now that they have begun to fear them. Tipped off, perhaps, by the arrest of some relative, resulting in their losing their party membership, the support they received as victims of SS persecution, their job, their home (Steinberger and Broggini, 28, 52ff.). No longer do they sit in the bright new apartments, built to humane proportions, or in the big buildings on the avenues, the successors of which will receive, much later, the pejorative name of block housing. Instead they sublet drafty rooms, a bed in the kitchen next to the coal oven. No more do they sit in the Hotel Lux, which housed the Communist International, with comrades from the world over. Instead they are in its backyard, in an old, unlit hovel known as the NEP Wing (Buber-Neumann, 15). The comrades who had remained friends with them no longer greet them; instead, they lower their eyes, walk to the other side of the street, from contempt, above all from fear.

They were supposed to be surrounded by friends: every neighbor a comrade, that was how they must have imagined it. At last, belonging to something more than a group of outcasts, no longer mistrustful of people on the street, of neighbors at the workbench, of shoppers in the stores. No more having to hide, like their comrades in Germany, Yugoslavia, Poland, Italy, the way they, too, had hidden, not so long ago; no more reading books in secret, carefully hiding them behind glued-on slipcovers; no more reassurances granted to detested authorities in public confessions (Weiss, 35). Now there hangs on the wall—or maybe it doesn't anymore, since they have already guessed at their imminent incarceration and refuse once again, this time in vain, to bow down—the portrait of the Great Comrade. Maybe one stands up one early afternoon in 1939, after sitting a long time silent at the kitchen table, goes over to the only framed picture in the sparsely furnished room, and takes it down. Possibly she holds it briefly in her hand, as if looking for something, as if she believed there was something there she could find, turns it around and sets it carefully next to the sink. She no longer has the strength for great gestures of rage. Around this time a few beams of light pierce the narrow window and fall shyly on the cupboard, on the stripes of the now completely bare walls. The white square remains visible on the wallpaper already darkened by the cheap coal oven with its eternally clogged flue: an angular emptiness, a free space apparently waiting for a new occupant. No one should ever have filled it—this much is clear now, far too late—the white square itself should never have been there at all.

Even those faithful to the party's supreme leader, even the most zealous of the Stalinists, are only very rarely safe from arrest. Without a trial, the arrested are condemned by an investigating judge, their confessions extracted through torture. The accusations speak of fascist "deviation," a critical attitude to Comintern politics, or sweeping conspiratorial relations with the National Socialist authorities, espionage (Articles 58, sections 6, 9, 10, and 11 of the RSFSR penal code), sympathy with Nazi Germany, a nation that virtually all of them had voluntarily declared themselves willing to fight against at the war's beginning, on the side, or better yet, as members, of the Red Army.

By this point, every attempt to locate an overarching rationality in the arrests and interrogations, in the guilty verdicts and banishments, even if only the irrational rationality of preserving authority, becomes blameworthy in its blamelessness, which grasping everything in expired concepts, overlooks the essential thing—the incomprehension, the debilitating rigidity the Communists lapsed into in their defenseless waiting. "At night, they waited for their own arrest. For weeks and months, the suitcase stood ready, the one that would accompany them to Siberia" (Buber-Neumann, 15).

Perhaps, like Vasso Millitsch, the character from a novel by Sperber (426), they carry out conversations with themselves as they await arrest, conversations in truth addressed to friends across the border, the long-deceased comrades who are the only ones capable of measuring the distance that separates the fall of 1939 from October 1917. To them and to them alone, to those with whom they shared the experience of revolution, the memory of that historically unique, world-spanning hope, could they convey the hopeless disappointment that has beset them. For a brief moment, they were granted, or at least caught a glimpse of, another life, the end of their history and the history of their ancestors—and then it was taken away. Perhaps nothing will ever compensate for this loss, certainly not in their brief lives or in any moment that has come after, all the way down to this very day. Rather the loss itself will become lost: for their successors, this loss will be the precondition of their existence, the basis of their political experience. Even with great effort, they will remain incapable of understanding revolutionary disappointment, though they, though we—all the way down to this very day—are the children, in the strict, historical, scientific sense, of this disappointment. The experience of this disappointment is not our own, but it does form us.

The Communists waiting in their dwellings to be arrested, in their cells for the next interrogation, in dark cages to be shipped to concentration camps, they know. That is why they converse with the dead, though their hopes are pinned on those born later, on others they will now never meet. With their lost comrades, they discuss their mistakes, their tactical omissions, or if they feel up to it, their clumsy, inspiring delusions, their fateful self-delusions most of all.

Unmitigated loneliness. Loneliness of the communists. Who will share their cell, their last walk out on the yard? Who will offer them companionship, who will step forward to be their ally? Who will bear witness for them? With whom is one to remember those who are only remembered as victims, who serve today only to bury, hand in hand with their murderers, the very hopes for which they were murdered? For often, the wrong people appear to mourn the victims of Stalinism. Appear to mourn— for they are not truly mourning. These dead whom the anticommunists lead to the battlefield are nameless, and if they were still alive, many of them would most likely refuse to be led. The dead cannot defend themselves. Probably they would have gone to the other side, to some other side perhaps (S. Leonhard, 5). Not in absolute numbers, naturally, but in relative ones, the victims of Stalinist terror came most often from their own ranks, and the danger was greater the closer they stood to the center. Party membership increased one's chances of arrest. They were communists. Who is to mourn them—as communists? Who if not the communists—whoever they may be? And yet the communists—most of them— are silent. The archives are open. But no broad or deep research has been undertaken, or very little, above all on the part of those who should be posing themselves questions most urgently (When? Where?), who should pose themselves questions without reprieve (How? Why?). Hardly any work of remembrance undertaken by those who most need to remember.[4]

No silence is permissible here, nor prevarication— prevarication perhaps even less so. No shameful, guilt-ridden covering over of the dead by those who—still trapped in the logic of the Cold War—take remembrance of the victims to be an anticommunist strategy or feel uttering their names to be the incantation of a procapitalist curse. In their fears, they feel stalked by an army of corpses marching beneath the banner of counter-revolution, determined to drag the last living communists down into their graves. In their blind defense of an allegedly real socialism, which was generally decent enough to refrain from using the *c*-word in the present circumstances, they endorse, with an authority they are as communists entitled to, their enemies' assertion that *this* is what communism was, and an alternative, if not the only alternative, to capitalism, to which, consequently, there is no real alternative (see S. Leonhard, 6). To the degree that *communists of the past* protect the past from attacks by a victorious present, they defend a temporarily victorious past as presented from the perspective of a present in which Stalin's head will forever remain welded to Karl Marx's cheek. They take the side of the party that liquidated their standard-bearers, position themselves behind the murderers who buried the revolution along with the murdered revolutionaries.

There may be no prevarication here and just as little, or almost as little, silence. A naively joyful continuation of the present, an ahistorical continuation of history by those who dream of a dream of a future that would be capable of redreaming itself, that could start from zero unburdened by the nightmares of the past. Free choice of a new terminology! Or even just a new name, an unsullied name for the project of a (properly something less than) all-embracing emancipation. As though a *new name* could accomplish more here than the simple affirmation of good, purified, best intentions. As though it could also change something about the dangers that live on under new names, unhindered by the caution that comes with the old ones. In their rhetoric of a break with the past, which they cannot break with, because they silence it, they do not even realize, these *communists of the present*, who as a rule do not call themselves communists, bolster their enemies' assertion that the End of History has already been reached, because for them *this* history is at an end. As though there were no predecessors, no combatants from before. But to bury the past's struggles for the future means nothing more, under the ongoing conditions of defeat, than burying the future itself—that is, another future. Wishing to keep their utopia free of past slaughters, of the revolutionaries' weapons that turned on the revolutionaries, they isolate their dream from the history of power and power struggles, isolate their utopia from the reality toward which it ought to strive. Uninterested in the revolution's victories, lionizing only those revolutionaries who perished before they could make it far enough, they confirm that all they want is to dream, not to triumph.

Both of them, Communists of the past and those of the present, betray again those communists the communists already betrayed. They prevaricate and silence anew those whom death had already silenced. They labor away at the fantasy of a guiltless posture, which yields to the illusion that it is possible to start over from the top, from zero, or simply go on in an unbroken line, liberated from the painful work of and on history. But in this case (as, perhaps, in all such cases), the flight from history turns ever in a circle.

2 Farewell

The thoughts which we are developing here originate ... [a]t
a moment when the politicians in whom the opponents of
Fascism had placed their hopes are prostrate and confirm
their defeat by betraying their own cause, these observations
are intended to disentangle the political worldlings from the
snares in which the traitors have entrapped them.
—Walter Benjamin, *Illuminations: Essays and Reflections*

Nineteen thirty-nine—fifty years before the official end
of socialism—the year the Russian Revolution dies its
last death. Many deaths will follow. Many precede it: the
Great Terror (1937–1938), the Show Trials (1936), deku-
lakization (1932–1933), the suppression of the Kronstadt
rebellion (1921), and so on. And it will rise again only
for three years, as a specter, the Red Army, in order to
destroy the German Wehrmacht, from 1943 to 1945.

Nineteen thirty-nine. The object is to call to mind
the historic moment of this event, of the coming of a
death foretold, its arrival of notice. To search for a place
where the tidings will ring loudest, will attain the greatest resonance, as if, for one historic hour, the entire city
was transformed into an audience, a resonant body, to
receive this message: Paris.

Here, at 44 Rue Le Pelletier, resides not only the leadership of the French Communist Party, the largest Communist Party in the Western world after the German Communist Party was destroyed, no, here thousands of communist and socialist immigrants who have fled from fascist Italy, National Socialist Germany, and most recently from Francoist Spain are standing by throughout the city and its many suburbs. Nothing, almost nothing but the struggle against fascism, holds them together in the United and Popular Fronts, which are finally endorsed in 1935 (S. Leonhard, 118). From the most far-flung places, from a multiplicity of struggles, they came here to wait, or so it seems, split up into groups, organize into café circles, often already feuding, eyeing one another up mistrustfully, made mutually dependent by emigration. As if they had gathered to say farewell.

Because this is the moment of farewell, the moment when the last, if not the very last, of these Communists who think for themselves are forced to recognize that a break with the party is unavoidable and cannot be postponed. And yet they do postpone it, incredulously they characterize the news as an invention of the bourgeois press, credulously they search for a dialectical explanation to account for what has happened, to neutralize the event, as so many have been neutralized before, by situating it within a strategy of sublation capable of undoing what has been done. But even as, still on summer vacation, they scorn the messengers as unworthy of belief, or when that no longer suffices, try to conceive of what has happened as a temporary, tactical maneuver, an artifice, a mere means to an end, the language of the message is too clear, too distinctive, for them to go on considering it a tactic indifferent to strategy, to keep affirming that even this time, the means will leave unblemished the end it allegedly serves.

Already on the morning of August 24, you can read it, see it, in all the papers. At the Moscow military airport, the swastika flag is hoisted to greet the German delegation, the Red Army orchestra plays the "Horst-Wessel-Lied." Stalin and Ribbentrop shake hands, smile for the camera, then the leader of the worldwide revolution and antifascism pronounces a toast to Hitler: "I know how much the German people love their leader, I drink to his health" (W. Leonhard, 15; Sperber, 606).

By signing the treaty, Stalin gives his imprimatur to a dynamic of escalation pursued by the Nazis and supported by the Western powers; he recognizes a constellation of imperialist powers that aggressively minimizes the Soviet Union's options for self-defense. Already during the negotiations for the Munich Agreement in September 1938, to which neither Czechoslovakia nor its ally, the Soviet Union, are invited, the French and British authorities signal their merely lukewarm opposition to National Socialist expansionism by conceding to Hitler's demand to annex the so-called Sudetenland to the German Reich. The Western powers responded with stalling tactics to Soviet entreaties in spring 1939, a response to the impending German invasion of Poland: the British government sent a low-ranking delegation to the negotiations in August; it traveled by ship despite the urgency of the occasion; it had no authority to act, could pledge no military aid, and above all was unable to answer the question of how the Soviet Union was to assist Poland when the Polish authorities withheld permission for the Soviet troops to enter. These conditions evoke and legitimize the Soviet view that the capitalist states are awaiting, if not even welcoming, a German war against the Soviet Union, so that a nonaggression pact appears one possibility of avoiding such a war. This perspective is shared by the later prime minister, Churchill (327), who soberly declares, "If, for instance, Mr. Chamberlain on receipt of the Russian offer had replied, 'Yes. Let us three band together and break Hitler's neck' … history might have taken a different course. At least it could not have taken a worse." From this perspective, the pact appears morally repugnant, but politically necessary, a cold, tactical calculation. Stalin himself appears to have believed the same. Even on the day of signing, he tells Khrushchev (150), "It's all a game to see who can fool whom. I know what Hitler's up to. He thinks he's outsmarted me, but actually it's I who have tricked him!"

The pact is meant to buy the Soviet Union time and space: time, because it delays the expected German attack by several years; space, because it extends the Soviet borders several kilometers further west, because as the secret amended protocol specifies, the Soviet Union's sphere of influence will extend into a number of countries: Finland, Estonia, Latvia and Lithuania, Bessarabia, Bukovina, and Eastern Poland. The Soviet Union plans to employ this time and space to prepare its defense, to push for militarization: but this time and space will be of no use to the Soviet Union, despite all efforts to make use of them, because the calculation that the war against England and France will decimate the Wehrmacht, and that it will not open a second front, does not bear out; because the new defensive lines are inadequately fortified and will crumble in a matter of weeks; because Russia's transfers of immense quantities of raw material to Germany will enable it to speed up and enlarge its war machine; because all the experienced Red Army generals and many of its officers have already fallen victim to the Great Terror (Hillgruber, 31; Zeidler, 93, Schmitt 44-45). Stalin will ignore precise warnings—from the spy Sorge, from Churchill, from Chiang Kai-shek—about the time and scope of Operation Barbarossa (Kremer, 22; Dimitroff, 392). On the day of the invasion, a large part of the material the Germans had promised will not yet have arrived; the armored cruisers the Germans committed to build will sit unfinished in the harbors, and as the Wehrmacht begins its invasion of the Soviet Union, it will cross paths with Soviet supply trains punctually crossing the border (Khrushchev, 258). Military relations between the Soviet Union and Germany will be worse in 1941 than in 1939 (Bühl, 18; Birkenfeld, 508f.).

On August 24, 1939, when they find out about the pact, through rumors or perusing the newspapers, the communists know none of this. They do not know and can only guess at the rationale of this tactical calculation taken by the narrowest circle of the Soviet leadership. They do not know and cannot know that another, secret accord accompanies the official one, an accord that will remain secret, in the Soviet Union, until 1989. Nor were they consulted, even informed, of the pact itself, of the preparations for it. And so almost no one is ready for the images of Ribbentrop shaking hands, of Stalin smiling for Hitler, almost no one is prepared for their sudden appearance—not the politburo, whose members are told of the agreement only briefly before and go hunting on the day of its signing; not the Comintern cadres, who hear mutterings at most; certainly not the run-of-the-mill comrades, who are stunned when they see the published photos (Khrushchev, 224; W. Leonhard, 24ff.). "For us," writes Ruth von Mayenburg, who is living in Russia at the time, "the clock at the Kremlin stopped" (W. Leonhard, 34).

The "shock of the Hitler–Stalin Pact" produces worldwide convulsions, tremors that span the globe, producing paralysis at first, and immediately afterward, rifts and factures (ibid., 1). The impact is felt initially— though it does not stop here—in the international

Communist Parties, especially in the United States and France; the latter, thanks to years of cooperation with social democratic and liberal forces, and the subordination of all political differences to the antifascist struggle, has grown from 40,000 to 270,000 members, and now finds itself objectively, and after a moment's hesitation, subjectively on the side of the German regime (ibid., 117). Then in the camps, the French ones, where after the declaration of war, the regime kept all immigrants, at least all immigrants perceived as male, confined as potential political enemies—in the famous Cépoy Camp, for example, where Heinrich Brandler, cofounder of the opposition KPO party, who "despite all criticism" continued to see in Stalin the "hope of the anti-fascists," registered a lasting change in the mood in favor of dissidents and against those loyal to the party line (ibid., 88). And so on in every country, in every place where discussion is possible, and in those where it appears impossible, in secret, whether in the Soviet Union or in the underground of the illegal resistance, in the penitentiaries, and in the concentration camps in Germany (ibid., 93ff.).

Inside the Brandenburg penitentiary, for example, which both the doctrinaire Erich Honecker and the dissident Heinz Brandt described in their memoirs. While the one asserts that the majority of imprisoned comrades were immediately pleased with the nonaggression pact and hailed it as a "diplomatic success," the other reports sharp divisions following the pact, a fatal

rupture of the solidarity that had once united the prisoners against the prison system (ibid, 88ff.). A rupture
that is in the Stalinist leadership's interests insofar as it
is based not only on a fundamental difference of belief
but furthermore arises and is processed in a specifically
authoritative form that makes it incompatible with political discussion. Because its source is a decision taken
without prior discussion, with no transparent basis, no
mutually agreed-on principles, all that its supporters
can cling to, the only thing preventing a leap to the opposition's side, is faith, obedience, blind trust. At the utter
mercy of the authorities, they feel hostility toward all who
doubt the infallibility of their fearless leader. Relinquish-
ing their entire capacity for judgment to the wisdom of
their overlord, they fall victim to regressive resignation
of a kind Leopold Spira (43) invokes succinctly in a single
phrase, "Stalin knows what should be done."

Two positions oppose each other mortally in the
appalling conditions of the Nazi penitentiary, two positions seeking an explanation for an inexplicable situation, each attempting to marshal historical analogies
to portray itself as the legitimate heir to the socialist
tradition. First by drawing an analogy between the nonaggression pact and the Treaty of Brest-Litovsk, which
saved the Soviet Union from an imperialist world war—
implicitly underplaying the economic and military progress of the Soviet Union, and explicitly relativizing the

differences between the bourgeois democratic and National Socialist varieties of capitalism. Second by drawing an analogy between the Hitler–Stalin Pact and the German Social Democrats' concession of war credits. Just like imperialistic nationalism betrayed pacifist internationalism, the security nationalism of Stalinist foreign policy betrayed the antifascist internationalism of the Third International.

Two antithetical positions—war or peace—which leave no room for mediation and yet did leave room for a multitude of the wavering, the undecided, who invested the nonaggression pact between the Germans and Soviets and the supplementary Frontier Treaty in September with a completely different, very concrete hope: a hope for full amnesty. Ignorant of the Soviet Union's transfer of thousands of prisoners to National Socialist Germany, whom they themselves could be exchanged for—not according to the nationalist logic of state citizenry, but rather to the political logic of the Communist International—they hope for release. Sitting in prison in Berlin, they hope the now *friendly* relations between the German Reich and the Soviet Union mean the international movement for the release of Ernst Thälman might finally make headway; they cannot know what Dimitrov (152–153), the general secretary of the Communist International, noted in his diary three months before the German invasion:

3-29-41: —V. M. [Molotov] has his doubts about the campaign in connection with Thälmann's fifty-fifth. If there is a conspicuous campaign abroad, while here we do not do a thing, that would be awkward. But having any kind of observance could hardly be politically expedient, since we are maintaining a nonhostile policy as regards the Germans.

Hardly politically expedient. Dimitrov's secret diaries, only published after 1990, speak openly of secret meetings in which, because they are secret, all secrets can be revealed, and what need no longer be kept secret from the enemy because, as a secret, it no longer exists. Antifascism, for example. If the Hitler–Stalin Pact had sprung from cool calculation, it would have had to disappear only in appearance, only to reappear cunningly—in the politics of the Communist International, which Moscow oversaw, in secret. But there is nothing to keep secret. The liberation of antifascist prisoners is not politically expedient, because expediency itself has stripped this mediocre politicking of purpose. Just six days after the beginning of the war, the great helmsman of the Communist International, who became famous in the Reichstag fire and played a key role in the change of course regarding antifascism at the Seventh World Congress, writes the following, obediently following Stalin's own analysis:[1]

9-7-39—At the Kremlin (Stalin, Molotov, Zhdanov).

Stalin:

—A war is on between two groups of capitalist countries—(poor and rich as regards colonies, raw materials, and so forth)—for the redivision of the world, for the domination of the world!

—We see nothing wrong in their having a good hard fight and weakening each other.

—It would be fine if at the hands of Germany the position of the richest capitalist countries (especially England) were shaken.

—Hitler, without understanding it or desiring it, is shaking and undermining the capitalist system.

—*The nonaggression pact is to a certain degree helping Germany.*

...—Communists in the capitalist countries should be speaking out boldly against their governments and against the war.

...—*The division of capitalist states into fascist and democratic has lost its former meaning.* (ibid., 115).

The division of capitalist countries into fascist and democratic ones has lost its former meaning—but it has also acquired a new meaning. Germany, England, and France are not equals in this "imperialistic, unjust war, for which the bourgeoisie of all the belligerent nations is equally responsible," but they are rather unequal in terms of raw materials, colonies, wealth, and poverty (ibid., 275). Poor Germany has gained socialist sympathy, an unwilling, unwitting agent of anti-imperialism whose struggle for "liberation from the Versailles system" weakens the leading empires and by doing so warrants assistance from the Soviet Union (ibid., 381).

This permits us to grasp the rationale behind the complete disappearance, from this point onward, of the concept of antifascism from Dimitrov's texts, in which the term appears solely as a disparagement of the "apostles of the anti-fascist war" (Keller, 28). From this point onward, we may explain, if not understand, Wolfgang Leonhard's observation that after the Hitler–Stalin Pact, antifascist literature disappears from Soviet libraries, antifascist plays and films like those of Lion Feuchtwanger are banned, and after the Border Treaty even Nazi newspapers suddenly are on display. What remains incomprehensible, because irreducible to any calculation of power politics, is Beria's order forbidding the guard staff in the gulags from disparaging political prisoners—antifascists in their majority, frequently convicted of "Trotskyite-fascist deviations"—with the epithet *fascist* (W. Leonhard, 74).

As if the dialectics of means and ends had undergone a historical deconstruction, the necessary border drawn between their poles becomes increasingly unstable, its inner hierarchies slip off toward uncertainty, tactical means break free of strategic ends until the two are transposed. A transposition of the international

proletariat and the national character of the sole workers' state, a transposition of disciplined revolution and
revolutionary discipline, a transposition of class and
party, of war and peace. This transposition is too powerful to be rescinded, reversed, rolled back from within by
those who form part of it. In this situation, clarification
from within, solidary critique from within the party-
established framework, are no longer possible. Amid
illegalization, nascent wars that pose a threat both to
the Soviet Union and the bourgeois states, complete
Stalinization, and the subjugation of party to apparatus,
the reversal of means and ends can no longer be halted,
let alone reversed from within. Only from without, only
through rupture.

And yet the communists reel and stumble, and their
awareness of their error, of their failures, weighs down
on them with the violence of a historical process in the
final stage of escalation. In fear, they withdraw from
this last step. The communists, who left their homeland
and their secure lives without hesitation, who have said
goodbye without hesitation to the beliefs handed down
to them, their families, their friends, and not seldomly
their comrades, now stall, hesitate to say goodbye to the
party. Seemingly without fear, they plunged into danger,
armed conflicts, prisons and torture chambers. Now
they are scared. Where does this fear come from? This
reticence? You lie once, no one believes you, but if you lie
too often, you even believe yourself—and yet the trope of

the dynamic becoming independent of its subject is not enough. It is not the habits that come with institutionalization that binds the communists to the Communist Party. They *want to believe*. They don't want to stop believing. They don't want to believe, cannot believe, cannot make themselves believe in the falsehood of what they believed in. For along with the past, which they call into question, the future too is cast into doubt—the very future to which they sacrificed the past. Along with the Communist Party, the future of communism becomes uncertain, too, the same future that had been certain as long as they had struggled for it on the side of the party. How then do they take leave of the party, which constitutes, guarantees, *is* their past and present, but also their future? Where else should they go, who should they ally with, who should they fight with, when it is the only thing there is? How should they leave it once politics has seeped into every second of their day-to-day life, when no friends exist but political friends, the ones the party approves, after they have broken off all contact with acquaintances, relatives, intimates, because there was no time left for them, no time permitted for them, last and not least because in this way, they were protected (Sperber, 202)? How then are they supposed to say goodbye to this last friend, to the great promise that loneliness would have an end?

But even when they do manage to take leave, when they do break with the party—in most instances because the party breaks with them—they don't take leave, not really, because there is no arrival for them, no place to come home to, nowhere they can count on a welcome. Now, enemies surround them. Cast out by their former comrades, threatened by armed henchmen of the apparatus, who infiltrate and control the emigrants, threatened by the old enemies, the capitalist International, the bourgeois anticommunists anxious for the Wehrmacht to march off to Moscow; threatened by fascism in Italy and Spain, threatened above all by National Socialism, which is expanding its borders and with them its grasp over those proscribed on its long lists: first Jews, then Sinti and Roma, then communists, antifascists. Even when they no longer position themselves on the side of the party, no longer serve the party, they still do not position themselves against it. Necessary as this may have been.

Sperber tells the fictional story of a group of communists hunted down by the party who hide out in Paris; intellectuals who have begun to publish, but have no place to publish, no one who cares to read their texts, no readers they can dare to imagine. It is raining one night in 1939, the water pounds on the glass pane of the skylight, the air raid siren grows louder and louder and drowns out the sound of the storm, when they receive an unexpected visitor. The person they open the door to is clearly exhausted, but even more than that, he is wary. Yet they are the first to be receptive to his stories—until then, no one he has told them to has believed him or even paid him any mind; they called him traitor, provocateur. The Czech communists in Prague, the émigré's section of the German Party, the PCF in Paris. The communists react as they almost always react to the unanimous reports of former gulag prisoners (Buber-Neumann, 416f.; Kuhn, 44ff.). They refuse to believe he has arrived there from a camp in northern Siberia, that he has fled his Soviet jailors, that he only managed to do so because a pardoned ex-captive, a dying Russian, gave him his name, and with it, his right to freedom. So he would leave, simply to report, simply to tell the world—the communist world, naturally, for none of this was supposed to get out. So he could call for help, demand the liberation of ten thousand comrades. Six hundred names of imprisoned communists, that was how many he should memorize; 563 he was able to recall. And he counts them off, all of them, while the exiles listen to his words, accompanied by the clatter of the rain on the skylight. The emigrants in Paris, party apostates, listen for hours to the names he rattles off—and they believe him. And yet they will not help, because they are incapable of doing anything for him or the prisoners from within the party. And they refuse to look for other allies, resist placing their trust in an only apparently neutral public. "The reason," one of them says after the messenger has finished, "has a name—Hitler" (Sperber, 549ff.).

The ostensible and obvious cynicism of their decision should not tempt one to disregard the cynicism of
this historical situation, particularly not in hindsight,
and this means here and now, especially after the German extermination camps, after Auschwitz, which was
neither imaginable nor foreseeable at the time. The
violence of their decision is embedded in the violence
of this historical situation, which suffuses the ideality of
every political or even merely ethical posture with a specific materiality. The materiality of the compulsion to
take a position in a dichotomous political field, the materiality of this dichotomy in a historically specific situation in which every decision must be weighed against
the question of whether or not it harms Germany. All
politics must pass through this gate, must submit to
this test, which grants a particular weight to a certain
idea, a slogan of Stalinism that long determined the
nature of confrontations, and—overlooked as it may
be—continues to do so to this day, even and especially
confrontations surrounding emancipation: criticism
hurts (cf. Kuhn, 22, 58, 83).[2]

Criticism hurts, that is also invoked by communists
of the present to lend a political rationalization to the
suppression of communists of the past. A spectral unity
of traditional communists and those lacking in tradition,
who strive to exorcize the specters of communists murdered by other communists in the name of communism.

For whom the remembrance of the victims seems to be in service of a neoliberal alliance of old powers whose theoretical weapon of totalitarianism is loaded with the ammunition of the memory of the dead. Unable to lay claim to the materiality of a comparable historical violence for their decision, they stress that Stalinist slogan which, however, they naturally feel to be the furthest thing from their understanding of their own nature, namely: criticism hurts.

Criticism hurts, that always comes up when the planes of struggle congeal into battle lines, the smooth, straight lines of warring sides that seamlessly converge. The dichotomous logic organizing the friend/enemy schema produces identitary effects on both sides, homogenizing the poles as it levels the space between them (cf. sinistra, 1). "There is no No Man's Land between the front lines; if you turn your face to one side, you will, without wanting to and without being able to prevent it, turn into the other's vanguard, the very ones it is absolutely imperative to kill" (Sperber, 445). "You don't stand between the barricades, you fall there, twice struck, twice killed" (ibid., 445). There is no no-man's-land between the lines or behind them, and no allied territory either. Only the singularity of one-dimensional space. Only loyalty and obedience to the party line.

But on the other hand, what can a text do—and if it had the better arguments, it would possess the weapon of a certain noncompulsory compulsion—against this powerful dynamic of power itself, which decodes it, no less urgently than compulsively, with a binary code? Who does such a text address, a text that imagines itself outside of the conflict of its addressees; a text that operates only in an imaginary outside of the "after" or "before," and—perhaps—can only operate within such a space? Nothing is easier than adopting a pacifist program—in times of peace.

How hopelessly naive is that aloof critique that once again opposes truth to power, however hopeful, however full of hope for a better world it may be. "It is not enough to die for mankind," one of Sperber's (23) communists replies to a Christian's moralizing criticisms, "you must kill for it."[3]

The critique of power, of the powerful, affirms—one's own—powerlessness. Motivated by the phantom of blamelessness, it can only sustain the confirmation of its moral superiority vis-à-vis the world through the confirmation of its separation from it. Even the most radical critique, which rejects every decision between false alternatives with reference to the forced circumstances that disclose their falsity, runs this danger. No wonder then that the *ethicization of the social* inevitably recurs when the opportunities for critique to have influence on history appear especially limited. So it was amid the conditions of post-Socialist trauma, after 1989. The retreat into the moral would then be—unconsciously—a double reaction to the failure of the communist movement. First to its final defeat, the worldwide erosion of borders by capitalist socialization, which retroactively gives every attempt at breaking free from it the appearance of futility; second, to its initial victory, its illusory success compared to its thousandfold mortal guilt the old raised forefinger (of the apostle of morality) has an exemplary, antiauthoritarian glimmer. It is the old calculation, innocence in exchange for powerlessness. But the calculation doesn't pan out. By presuming to decide on the moral validity of a decision while disregarding the conditions under which this decision was taken, the ethicization of the social imagines a freedom the absence of which is precisely what is at issue, looks away from the very thing that is crucial: history. People decide, but not under freely chosen conditions, rather under ones that befall them. The communists know that. Neither the choice of weapons nor the choice of morality is without preconditions. In sober definitions of external conditions—or in hasty obedience to them—everything, for them, depends on the historical constellation. In this case, in this singular situation, the rise of National Socialism appears to determine this constellation completely. Even if it is the result of historical processes to which the communists, as historically engaged subjects, are coresponsible to a not inconsiderable degree—the failure of the 1918–1919 revolution, the collapse of the German worker's movement in 1933—everything else must now be set aside for the sake of the struggle against it. These are the conditions

that must be reconstructed, and that govern the decision to side with the party or oppose it—the conditions
under which the communists choose wrongly when they
choose not to break with Stalinism. They constitute the
materiality of a binary logic from which one cannot easily emerge, not without fault, the consequences of which
may be traced back to the historical turning points at
which they turned against themselves—at which the
party turns on its partiality.

3 Party

The cryptic diplomacy of the future.
—Georg Glaser, *Geheimnis und Gewalt*

It starts with: dreams are for those who cannot endure,
who are not strong enough for reality; it ends with: reality is
for those, who are not strong enough to endure, to confront
their dreams.
—Slavoj Žižek, *The Pervert's Guide to Cinema*

In 1937, that long year "that begins with the first Moscow Show Trial in August of 1936 and lasts until the last Show Trial in March of 1938," the October Revolution celebrates its twentieth—its last—anniversary; in 1937, amid the roar of the Great Terror, the Russian Revolution founders, drowns with a nearly bureaucratic frenzy, chokes on—itself (Schlögel, 50). Independently of where it came from, independent of when exactly it began, the counterrevolution now attains its final triumph. Because it is, without a single doubt, a counterrevolution that reaches its conclusion in that year. It is such because it brings the revolution to an end, buries the last vestiges of it, buries first of all, above all, the revolutionaries themselves. Of the 1,966 delegates to the Seventeenth Party Congress, the Congress of Victors, in 1934, 1,108 of them are imprisoned, disappeared, shot, buried after not even five years; of the 139 party secretaries listed in the 1936 Directory for Moscow and the surrounding area, only 7 remain in office (Montefiore, 148; Schlögel, 50). In 1937, the Red Army loses more officers than any army before in peacetime, the exiled Japanese Communist Party is decimated, as is its German counterpart, the Polish party is thoroughly liquidated. In Leningrad, the capital of the revolution, as in the rest of the Russian Soviet Federative Socialist Republic (SFSR), 90 percent of all party cadres are locked up, "the bugs' nests of the Trotskyite-fascists" are smoked out and destroyed (Werth, 215). The counterrevolution is exhaustive. From Voronezh, the party functionary Andrey Andreyev telegraphs Moscow: "Here, the politburo no longer exists. All cadres have been imprisoned as enemies. Now back to Rostov" (Montefiore, 290).

Without a doubt, it is the Stalinist counterrevolution that "liquidates" the revolution, to employ a word loved by both, and at the same time, it surely is not. At no point does this counterrevolution declare itself to be a counterrevolution, at no point does it declare war on the achievements of the revolution; indeed, what it declares war on is the counterrevolution. Not from without does it strike the "socialist homeland," but from within, from the headquarters of the regime, from the center of the party. It organizes no military putsch, summons no allied troops from other countries, but rather "unmasks" on its own, constantly, tirelessly, the omnipresent conspirators, spies, agents of enemy powers. It marches not under the white banner, but under the red. And it fights not in the name of order, of freedom, of the market, but in the name of the revolution, of socialism, of plans.

For it was planned, the great wave of terror, centrally, bureaucratically. A state socialist terror plan, just as precise and just as imprecise as state socialist economic planning. On July 30, 1937, Order Number 00447 is issued. It demands the arrest of 332,400 people, divided into two categories: 259,450 who are to be imprisoned for eight to ten years (Category 2) and 72,950 who are to be executed (Category 1) (ibid., 263; Werth, 187). Repression, like production, should be carried out according to quotas. And the quotas, as always in the realm of the brave Stakhanovite workers, will be exceeded. In this socialist competition the cadres outdo each other to prove their diligence. A certain Khrushchev, for example, later renowned as an anti-Stalinist, orders the execution of 55,741 suspects in response to a quota of 50,000.

Soon, after just one month, the regional cadres demand an increase in their respective quotas, soon other orders succeed Order Number 00447, after the "liquidation of the former kulaks, criminals, and other anti-Soviet elements" comes the "liquidation of criminal elements," and then the "liquidation of families of enemies of the people" (Werth, 191). When the wave of terror runs down,

1,345,000 people have been sentenced, 681,692 of them to death (ibid., 190–191). These judgments, representing 85 percent of all death sentences handed down during the Stalinist era, are carried out during the festivities marking the twentieth anniversary of the revolution. Accompanied by parades and merrymaking, framed by radiant banners: "Life has become better, life has become more cheerful" (Stalin) (Buber-Neumann, 10).

The terror, centrally planned, but decentrally energized, constantly intensifying—in which, according to Yezhov, the head of the NKVD, "a thousand more"—no fewer—don't matter, in which the executioners must expect to be executed if they demonstrate "flagging commitment," but may be rewarded if they fulfill their duties "selflessly" and in record time; at many of Moscow's execution sites, from Communarka to Butovo, up to 562 per day are killed (Schlögel, 49; Wehner, 11). Vertiginous, mounting terror, the experience of which can hardly be relayed, because its sheer boundlessness exceeds every biographical dimension. The experience of which can only be relayed, perhaps, by the hangmen themselves, the shooters, the secretaries, the torturers. Because at least they survive longer, for a year, for two years, for a long time, even, and because their exhaustion at least offers a way to measure the immeasurableness of their deeds. Not the psychological burdens they cannot—or can—endure (that would be all too human), but the overtaxing of their bodies—up to 400 "*cases*" checked off per day, up to 50 confessions obtained under torture per night, weariness, muscle cramps, tendinitis in their trigger fingers (Wehner, 11; Schlögel, 51). Diagnosis: executioner's arm.

The Great Terror, the greatest wave of terror the Soviet Union would know, which ends, on Stalin's orders, in 1938, has already begun in December 1934 with the murder of Kirov, which, regardless of who committed it, becomes the trigger for vengeance and purging, and already by 1935, leads to the expulsion of 250,000 party cadres, 9 percent of all members of the party (Werth, 182). Before the wave even breaks, later ones wash over it, each overreaching the other, a purge of waves upon waves, the undertow dragging down the purgers themselves, turning perpetrators into victims. The regional party leaders, after unmasking all the enemies of the party, after ridding themselves of all dangers, will themselves become dangerous as their power grows, dangerous and hence enemies of their party. And those who give the orders are followed by those who implement them, all the way down to the agents of the NKVD. Their leader, Yagoda, will be relieved of his duties and shot in September 1936, in the early phase of the Great Terror—and with him, another 3,000 Chekists. He is followed by his erstwhile assistant, Yeshov, who will give his name to the Great Purge—the *Yezhovshchina*. With its end comes his downfall, at the same time, in November 1938. Stalin no longer needs him, yet Yeshov remains true to

Stalin. To the very end, when he is shot, even beyond the very end. In his final letter, Yeshov writes, "Tell Stalin I will die with his name on my lips."

Those are not helpless victims who move us to identify with them and hence to spare them compassion. Such people may exist, but not among the Communists, not anymore, not here or now. There may be some, but only where they were pulled off the train, where they stood on the wrong street, at the wrong station, dreamily absorbed in the pattern of the paving stones. Certainly there are some once the list of the NKVD's enemies runs out, and for the sake of quotas, new ones must be found, invented, among the hostile ethnic groups, the national contingents, perhaps, among the Romanians, the Finns, the Lithuanians, the Greeks, or the Turks. And certainly they exist among those whose activities make them suspect, and are presumed to be participants in a conspiracy: members of the Esperanto club, those employed at the time of a factory fire, those with pen pals overseas, even stamp collectors. It is enough to live near the border or to be standing, by chance, in the path of a raid (Schlögel, 51; Werth, 177). Susanne Leonhard (95) tells of a Tartar kolkhoz farmer she met in Butyrka who only speaks Russian poorly:

She returned from her first interrogation in a rage. ... "[T]he band of liars," the Tartar cursed. "I'm supposed to just sign a confession for things that never even happened." "What is it, Tonya, what's not true." "The thing with the tractor. My uncle came and said I should learn to drive a tractor, his daughter-in-law is learning too, and it can help a person get ahead. But I said I'd rather stick with the cows, I can do that, you can get ahead with that just as well. I told him again I don't want to deal with the tractor, and so I didn't go. And now I ought to confess that I was a tractorist or Trotskyist or however you're supposed to say it."

The confession that nothing can be confessed, because there is nothing to be confessed, the confession of not knowing what there is to be confessed. "The secret, the perplexity of the year 1937," Karl Schlögel (49) writes, "consists still in the blindness of the context of violence." And this blindness is evident in the lack of criteria for the arrests and the imperviousness of the interrogations and trials to judicial argumentation, protestations of innocence, gestures of submission. Only a few weeks, a few days between arrest and a verdict issued in a matter of minutes, which seems to retain the lineaments of a judicial proceeding—interrogation, confession, declaration of guilt—only out of habit, a bureaucratic habit without a bourgeois tradition (Werth, 189). "Without an awareness of the helplessness of the situation, those born later will be incapable of comprehending this era, which is in the past but has still not become history. The confusion is summed up in the questions that those affected that year asked themselves over and over without finding an answer: Why? To what end? Why me? It is not simply a question of investigating the number of victims, but also of a logic, an inner *ratio*, a so-called rational core, which any history writing that aims for an explanation cannot dispense with" (Schlögel 49). If there were a rationality writing this history, if a political rationality could be found within this history, it would undoubtedly lie in the party, that 2-million-strong organization in a state of 170 million people, which shapes not only the interior of this historical process but also its central concepts. The party, which reaches past itself to deploy its logic over the entire societal field, in order to constitute it as a terrain of struggle in which it will turn on itself.

This self-destruction of the party appears to destroy not only the party but also partisanship, not only the specific socialist one—partisans on the side of the oppressed—but with it—if there is such a thing—the general sort, partisanship itself. Because it can affect and does affect all without distinction, the lower, the middle, the higher cadres, enemies and affiliates of the party, members as well as neutrals, it submits its destructiveness to no criterion beyond nonpartisan wantonness. No class corresponds to its—open to all interpretations—classification of enemies to be liquidated (workers, peasants, soldiers, relatives), no political rank, no bureaucratic post is spared. A postparticular, universal terrorization of society; equalization that turns to leveling as it is sucked up into the accelerating vortex and that retains, when it comes abruptly to a standstill, only a single zone of stillness, an eye of the storm, consisting of a tiny number of heads (Stalin + x). Its irrationality undermines the classic logic of terrorism itself, for what can be the point of propagating comprehensive fear throughout society when even the unremitting commitment to authority, the purest identity of Stalinist identification, brings with it no security?

Observing from within, one does not, cannot recognize what meaning these persecutions might have. Unable to draw on the broad view subsequent perspectives allow, unable to at least ask for another explanation, however late it is in coming, the insistence on inner logic of political rationality poses the same old questions (Why? What for? Why them?) and seems capable only of repeating the same old lack of answers, the same dead-ends. As if socialist purges, suspicion of guilt, and self-criticism were comprehensible without taking into account not only the Christian tradition in general but also the specifically Russian Orthodox practice of public confession. As if clan liability could be understood without the patriarchal tradition of patronage systems. As if it were possible to understand state socialism and the actually existing "dictatorship of the proletariat" without analyzing the political rationality of sovereignty and capitalist biopolitics, without a critique of the logic of monarchical and bourgeois state forms. As if the destructive dynamism of Soviet society could be understood without recourse to violent collectivization of the agrarian revolution, this retained primitive accumulation, the expulsion of millions upon millions of peasants that forms the basis of urbanization and industrialization. As if the logic of a proletarian party could be grasped without reference to the reconstitution of the urban proletariat, which had been decimated in war and civil war, without reference to the doubling of Moscow's population in the matter of a decade. As if it were possible to explain the widespread practice of denunciation without mentioning interinstitutional competition, the possibility of upward mobility through the replacement of elites, above all to the unresolved scarcity of dwellings. As if an analysis of historical materialism transformed into historical power could succeed without reflecting on its material conditions, without economic analysis. (The same economy that should be placed within the political realm opened up by socialism, but that bureaucratic centralization constantly reproduces as a base—a base that in the manner of an alien object, eludes all attempts by the political superstructure to subdue it.) As if the arbitrariness of the arrests could be grasped without understanding the extreme pace of state capitalization, with "interior colonies" in the gulag system, former camps for political prisoners now transformed into forced labor camps, which develop an insatiable demand for slave labor, and that in the absence of exterior colonization and its corresponding racist ideology, necessarily give a different political form to the acquisition of labor power. As if the political irrationality of Stalinism were decipherable without the codex of the economic rationality of disciplined productivity, the capitalist imperative that speaks out unaltered within state socialist politics as the systemic unconscious.

But the exit that an exteriority represents harbors within itself—danger and temptation—the tendency to overwrite responsibility for the failure of communism, the tendency to banish the possibility of it happening again either with reference to the unrepeatable specifics of the historical situation or with reference to the unabated power of the eternal enemy. The stress on the unaltered continuity of dominion, as well known as it is struggled against, works to cover over the rupture in spite of which and in which it continues to exist. This perspective obstructs the view of continuing possibilities for collaboration, of the specific ways—different from yet comparable to those of social democracy—that socialism merges with capitalism. It tends to assign all crimes to a stylized other, and in this way serves up a guilty defense that constitutes a leftist subject freed of any deep-seated relationship to the failures and crimes of its forbears. We are (and always were) the good ones. But the truth is paradoxical. No, that wasn't communism. But at the same time, it wasn't not communism.

The responsibility of clarifying the question of why the attempt at liberation turned into the most gruesome despotism falls not on the monarchist counterrevolutionaries, on the Whites, not even on the capitalists, but on the communists. For even if the old domination had merely lived on unchanged under a different name, the question would still remain: why and how it was able to live on so murderously, why did these odious names not impede it. From the perspective of communism, which asks how the future can avoid being a repetition of the past—one past or the other—the question arises, must arise, of why communism, "the real movement, which sublates the current state of things," has not sublated the current state of things (but rather, a previous one in the present) (Marx and Engels a).

Observed from within, from a place where, admittedly, only an incomplete, skewed view is possible, as this essay, this failing attempt, continuously demonstrates, it is apparent that the communists participate in the purges not only out of fear but also enthusiastically; that they denounce not only as an individual survival tactic but rather in service to a collective party strategy. From the perspective of the inner logic of the party and its processes, which can do no more than perpetuate its lack of logic, its illogicality, it becomes clear that those obedient to the authorities and the apparatus, to the leadership and its police, are compelled not only by fear but also by conviction, by a sense of socialist duty. The dynamic of an almost complete self-destruction grinds on with revolutionary energy.

Nineteen thirty-six. Initiated before the first show trial, and realized just a few weeks afterward, the assembly of the German section of the Union of Soviet Writers in Moscow takes place. It is a closed assembly in four sessions, not so much four days as four late nights between September 4 and 9, a meeting that takes the form of a circle, because the current prohibition on political groups means no one dares to call a meeting of party cells for fear of possible "guilt-by-contact" or allegations of "association" (R. Müller, 445). Eyes ringed with red, the communists meet for their nightly gatherings, timid, fearful, and at the same time soldierly, prepared, ready to obey. Though the official session leader makes it clear that this is not a *chistka*, a purge, it is hardly something else; the comrades, who must literally step forward, one after the other, into the middle of the assembly, confess their activities past and present, even those from long ago, confess above all their shortcomings, their unpardonable failings. Exhausted, they confess, well into the wee hours of morning, their lack of vigilance, their moments of deviance. Then the questions begin, one by one around the group, the comrades should and must query, needle, interrogate: everything is carefully stenographed for the NKVD, which gratefully accepts the material for the upcoming prosecutions. In this "highest form of democracy," in this "moving" and "salutary procedure, which penetrates to the deepest human layer," as Inge von Wangenheim will regard the purge as late as 1954, everyone must "confess, discuss, give an account" of their "lives," their "humanity," their "responsibility." "There were no questions that couldn't be asked, and no questions that did not have to be answered"—except, of course, for the question about the point of all these inquiries, the question of whose interests these questions were asked in, and who stood at the unquestionable center, categorically free from questioning (ibid., 20f.). Institutionalized questioning turns the critical power of the question against the possibility of critique. But the purview of questioning, in the practice of the purge, is nevertheless rather restricted. The political writers hardly talk about politics, or only do so in a highly personal way; they talk about people they have met, acquaintances, relatives, friends, and comrades in the daily struggle, whom they attempt to wash themselves clean of now, when they have suddenly fallen into disgrace. They would have preferred to have always known, to have picked up on it sooner, better still, to have smelled it. With their "nose" for politics, they would like to have noticed that something wasn't right, that these people's "homoerotic relations," for example, rendered them suspect (ibid., 455, 399, 414f.). And yet they cannot help it, they must confess—to themselves, to their comrades, to the leadership—that they didn't always know, that they noticed these deviations far too late, that they were honestly shocked to see the great heroes unmasked as Trotskyite-Zinovievian conspirators, as Gestapo agents, as fascists, in brief. "Right in our midst, shoulder to shoulder with us sit the enemies, and we do not see, we almost do not believe in this possibility until this trial unfolds before us," Emma Dornberger, a participant in the purge meetings, writes in her diary a few months before her own imprisonment (ibid., 53). They do not see, or see too little, for this reason they are guilty or in need of reform; they must learn to see more, even that which cannot be seen, even the unseeable.

Lukács, the philosopher, the Stalinist Lukács, proffers the epistemological pretext:

I believe a thoroughly new problem reveals itself in the question of vigilance, the outlines of which were already present in the Kirov trial, but which now appears with absolute clarity. Previously, the enemies of the party came forward with a specific ideological platform. We were able to analyze: this person is a Bukharist, a Trotskyist, etc. The present enemies of the party have no platform, but rather appear in the disguise of party faithful. (ibid., 184f.)

But it would be too simple to simply call Stalinists those "one ... used to call warships," those never tainted by the suspicion of "opposing the party line," those who never gave a speech "without beginning and ending with Stalin" (ibid., 185). The truth, understandably, is more complicated. It demands a specific epistemological method in order to recognize the oppositional essence behind the appearance—the mere, the false appearance!—of opportunism. "Unmasking these people requires a complicated vigilance" (ibid.). Vigilance to the point of sleeplessness, of dreamlessness. It is complicated because it turns no longer on practical politics, not even on political positions, but rather on thoughts that elude the conscience, on fleeting errors. "The writer thus" in this case *"falls victim to the most* dreadful terrorism, *the jurisdiction of suspicion"* about which the young Marx soberly remarks, "Better like that Russian Tsar to have everyone's beard cut off by Cossacks in his service than to make the state of mind due to which I wear a beard the criterion for the cutting" (Marx and Engels a, 1, 14; emphasis in original). But the red czar responds, "Behavior inimical to the party begins not with sabotage, but with doubts as to the correctness of the party's direction. There are too many fault-finders, and they must be wiped out." Anyone who dares, "even in thoughts, yes, in thoughts!" to weaken Soviet power "will be wiped out with his entire clan" (Montefiore, 280).

Stalin is this one-dimensional, but the Stalinists are not. Lukács, the philosopher, the Stalinist Lukács, may well speak "more about general questions than about personal ones," from a "highly objective ground" such as befits a philosopher—because he alone, among all those present, is not a member of this communist organization, not a member of the German section of the Union of Soviet Writers—nonetheless, he speaks, and stressing this is something he feels strongly about, he speaks "in the majority," "not in the pluralis majestis, but rather in the first place from that guilt that I bear." The communists bring charges, not only against those who left a propaganda event in support of the show trials twenty minutes before the end, before the thundering wave of applause; not only against those who sent warm underwear to a Trotsykist imprisoned in a Siberian camp; but above all against themselves (R. Müller, 96ff., 157, 15).[1] The libidinal economy of Stalinism, which clusters around the phantoms of purity, of cleanliness, reacts against filth and muck, foul language and smut, sexual excess and deviance, appears to thrive on the lust for denunciation, on punishment, as well as on the lust for confession, for self-subordination (ibid., 92).

In September 1936, in the first of the four purge sessions of the German section of the Union of Soviet Writers, comrade Hans Günther has his turn to exercise self-criticism for a mistake he committed in March 1933. His is a repeated self-criticism, for already at the time he "offered an immediate public self-criticism to all relevant parties concerning the entire incident," did not simply take this mistake—his only mistake in recent years, as he repeats numerous times—lightly, but rather suffered for it: "I have truly looked deep into my soul and have viewed my entire party activity since that moment as, in a certain sense, a labor necessary in order to atone for this error" (ibid., 101). It must have been a grave error indeed to demand such a labor of atonement and yet still be unredeemed three years later, regardless of this work. What was this grave error then? Günther had considered the party's participation in the Nazi-instigated referendum against the Prussian Social Democratic Party (SPD) a mistake, had seen the National Socialist takeover in 1933 as a defeat for the working class, a defeat for the party.

An untenable posture that cannot be allowed to continue, and that moreover will not continue, "no longer than 4 days," to be exact, 4 days that comrade Lukács needs in order to convince Günther that this posture is nothing more than "a kind of mood," a "depressive mood" (ibid., 97). A depressive mood that—this is Lukács's decisive argument—when thought through "politically to the end" and elevated "to a political platform," necessarily terminates in "opposition to the party" (ibid., 117). For that reason, the critique was wrong in 1933 and remains wrong in 1936, when the party is forced to conclude, at the Seventh World Congress of the Communist International, that the Nazi seizure of power represented an unequivocal defeat for the working class, if not precisely for the party itself. The critique, then, had been *unclear*, *exaggerated*, *premature* (ibid., 98). Günther himself lays the greatest stress on this: "The fact that the 7th World Congress took place must not interfere with my self-criticism" (ibid., 101).

But prescribed self-criticism isn't self-criticism. Any more than a person given the choice of shooting herself or being shot can be said to commit suicide. It's that simple. But it is not so simple to distinguish the "cruelly thorough" self-criticism of Marx from the thoroughly cruel self-criticism of Stalin, which relies on this semantic inheritance to constitute itself as self-criticism. Just as the question can be both a technique of subversion and of interrogation, so self-criticism may be the form through which not liberation, but despotism, imposes itself more perfidiously, more perfectly, than in other forms. History has demonstrated this, and it remains a latent danger, because self-criticism can never, and may never, derive its critical standards from within itself, because critical engagement precedes it from without and is addressed—like an open letter—to an exterior; to the self, but only before witnesses. And there is nothing that might aid one to stave off the possible survival of despotism in this critique except vigilance, were it not itself a Stalinist concept.

In 1935, only shortly before the KPD declares the united front policy its official party line, Sperber situates the story of a communist in the antifascist underground whose experience of the minuscule and steadily dwindling resistance to the *Volksgemeinschaft,* the National Socialist people's community, compels him to revise the analysis of the central party organization across the border in Prague, affirming that so-called social fascism remains the greatest enemy. In the face of massive arrests and a change of tone among the German workers, who suddenly realize, in accordance with their new ethos, that they are Germans first and workers second, he begins to cooperate on the local level with deviant communists, even with social democrats. A grave offense from the perspective of the party, particularly in bad times like these; and for deviations the times are always bad. Hard times; above all, it is hard for an illegal party to organize an orderly disciplinary proceeding like excommunication from the party. But since those excluded from the party, those who oppose the party line, are automatically against the party and on the side of its enemies, the apparatus opts for an approach practicable under the circumstances: betraying the communists to the Gestapo. Even in the concentration camp, like other unwilling renegades, he is rejected by his communist comrades as a traitor (Buber-Neumann, 224, 236).

It takes a special sort of party dialectic to justify this proceeding, and the leader of the Communist Party, who legitimated the apparatus's approach, even if he didn't initiate it, has such a thing in his power:

"It's true he saw things completely right, but he acted wrongly. I recommend the entire line (on account of which he was dispatched) but he attempted to pursue his line over the head of the party."

"But if his line was correct?"

"It wasn't, because it wasn't the Party's line. Perhaps tomorrow it will be, if the Party takes it up and makes it into its own." (Sperber 218)

Revolutionary discipline, antifascist in this case, until the point that antifascism comes into conflict with discipline—and buckles under. Loyalty to the party and its line even where this objectively—but naturally only temporarily, from a tactical perspective—is wrong. Unconditional obedience, justified only on the pretext that the party alone can successfully wage revolution, that it alone is in the position to effectively organize the antifascist resistance. But the political justification cannot be sustained even according to its own criteria. The centralistic party, formed according to the Leninist model, which proved—formally—victorious under czarism, is largely ineffective in the struggle against a technologically superior and culturally united National Socialism. The constant smuggling of information and newspapers over the borders, necessary for the leadership in Prague or Moscow to command and coordinate actions in the German underground, but above all to ideologically accompany, safeguard, permeate it, is both dangerous and extremely unproductive measured against the goal of sabotaging the NS machinery. As opposed to, for example, individual acts of terrorism, which the Communist Party condemns. Handing out flyers, still the

Communist's preferred course of action even after the ban on protests—and not seldom a suicidal one, given the successful mobilization of the people's community (*Voksgemeinschaft*)—is based on a catastrophically trivializing analysis of fascism that never breaks from the vision of National Socialist workers as socialists led astray who can be won back through the right propaganda. Limited antifascism, then, a weak legitimation of inner terror, of party terror in contrast to individual acts of terror, which are shunned. But plausibility of the imperative never to criticize the party, let alone abandon it, is based, especially for left-wing intellectuals, on an argument on a completely different level from the tactical or strategic one. On the epistemological level.

Against the background of a long tradition of Marxist critique of philosophy, which reveals assertions of objective truth standing outside power relations—outside the class struggle, in other words—to be bourgeois ideology, the party represents a consistent, practical critique of ideology. It gives rise to a theory-practice node, an inextricable binding of subject and history, of truth and power, by which the marginalized truth of the oppressed, which otherwise remains mere opinion, fleeting accusation, private protest, can accede to historical power. It is an epistemological pragmatism, methodological positivism on the terrain of the philosophy of history: history will answer the question of truth, the hypothesis of revolution must be historically verified.

And it was historically verified, it came true in the form of the Soviet Union. The point is to understand the nature of the authority, the immunity to criticism that accrues to the Russian Revolution and its concomitant institutions through the simple fact of its victory and its—historically unprecedented—defense of them. The argumentative force of its mere existence is necessarily significant for a materialist. Measured against it, every argument, every speech, every text becomes cerebral, disembodied, in short: idealistic. This makes comprehensible the often redoubled crippling of the international communists, whose revolutionary attempts in Germany and elsewhere were not so much successful as resounding failures. If, as Peter Weiss notes, they could not even achieve an eight-hour workday, how could they dare to teach lessons, give advice, to the USSR and its leadership in Moscow?

The historical force of this binding of truth and power, and the advance payment of faith it draws on, must be understood by anyone who wishes to grasp why the communists are sparing with critique, why they hesitate, almost always for too long, to withdraw their faith from that which, for the first time in history, speaks the language of those whose language was taken from them.

The party, which speaks the language of the workers, offers itself as a speaking tube through which the formerly speechless may enter into dialogue with history.

A history that, for the most part, has repeated the same monologue endlessly, the prevailing monologue, the monologue of those who have prevailed. They refuse to give their vote, their voice to bourgeois democracy, yet, for the right to a vote, to a voice, or the right to speak and be heard, they are willing to cast their vote—even, perhaps, to cast it aside. That is the trade-off, the deal they enter into, which concludes when they join the party. The prospect of communist discourse in exchange for the renunciation of critical participation in the discourse of the Communist Party. As if it were necessary, as if it were even possible to carry out, even to begin, a communist conversation when silenced in this way. But they believe—not always, even perhaps only rarely because they truly believe that in a Communist Party, the word must always come from above, with many ears for one mouth. No: they do so because they are aware of the weight of this historically specific nexus, because they know how many strings come together to make this knot and how little remains outside it. *What* is the question that the critics of the party, the dissidents, those already excluded, and those who have fled keep hearing over and over: *What can you offer us instead?* In a formulation of which the above-cited dictum of the German Party leaders is only the grim continuation, they ask what truth there is outside the party, what significance this truth might have without the party. What worth does truth have without power?

And so it is not only the leadership that demands discipline and unity within its ranks; unity is not mandated only from above but also longed for from below. More so, even. The base, which the communists (with the exception of the upper party cadres, who gladly transfer their own responsibility to the base when it comes to taking responsibility for past defeats) seem almost naturally inclined to reconstitute as the logical continuation of the masses, the oppressed, *those from below*, wants—or as at least a great deal of research indicates as such—one thing above all: unity. Unity of class against capital, unity of social democrat and communist workers, unity—later—of international and national socialists.[2] Irrespective of tactical correctness in the individual instance, which may mean everything, as in the united front policy against the Nazis, the socialist everyday religion of the *little "man"* sacralizes unity into a fetish decoupled from historical struggles. What the so-called base then longs for in its insistence on the community of the like-minded might be tantamount to a demand to carry out on a larger scale, with greater scope, what the parties, the communist one in this instance more so than the Social Democrats, enforce within their own ranks: homogenization, discipline, refusal of disagreement, liquidation of the opposition. Without equality, there can be no unity. And equality that strives for unity is not equality in the emancipatory, communist sense. Rather the opposite: though unity, drawing on the experience of the capitalist economy, signifies unity against the competition, which, according to Marx, is the "sole basis of wage labor," the fetish of equality itself can be analyzed as a replica of the capitalist money and commodity fetish (Marx and Engels a, 473). Just as the one can only process the relations among different use values through reduction and quantification, so the other can only process the relations among different political systems through homogenization and hierarchization.

And at the same time, unity in equality is not gridlock, not a zero-sum game of mere equivalencies. It also yields an added value, or promises to do so. A symbolic surplus value and moreover a historical surplus value extending beyond biography. The surplus value of transcendence, of survival.

"And yet one was alive," Sperber (177) allows one of his communists to think in the moment of greatest exhaustion, in expectation of his own death, "and so the Party was alive. And it didn't die with those it lived inside of. Because there were always more."

The party lives. And as it doesn't die with those it lives in, instead they live, survive, through it, in it. In the party's organizational metaphorics, the organization is more than just an instrument for the abrogation of power, it is a living organism that feeds on the lives of its members, who provide it with a part—the greater part—of their vital energy. They trade the prospect of an early death, a reduction of lived time, for entrance into, ascent into, this greater life that extends out beyond, outlives, its component parts. The party doesn't die with those it lives in, but it does live, now and then, from those who die for it. It outlives those who live through it, and there are times when circumstance demands it survive at the expense of those who must die. Even when they manage to follow the abrupt twists and turns of the party line, the party's interwoven lifelines, they burn out, use themselves up, atrophy from cadre to cadaver, bodies rendered useless, who may do the party one final service by disposing of themselves voluntarily.

In a Moscow remand prison, a GPU agent interrogates a leading cadre of the Communist Party. It is necessary to quote at length from this interrogation, as Sperber (394, 395ff.) describes it:

"I'm not playing along. At the trial, I will say why I am against Stalin, why I believe that despite the planned economy, despite collectivization, with every step you have moved away from the revolution, from socialism, and have become an Asiatic tyranny, from 1927 on [when Trotsky left the party], and ..."

"Wait, wait, you are getting off the subject. Since 1927, then, you have seen through these mistaken policies and yet have embraced them without resistance, yes or no?"

"Yes."

"And this was so right down to the day before your imprisonment, yes or no?"

"Yes."

"You sent people to battle, to jail, to the camps, even to their deaths while following such policies, yes or no?"

"Yes."

"And now, in line with these policies, another comrade must die, but it happens that this comrade is you, and all of the sudden it occurs to you that things can't go on this way. Thousands of comrades die, and it's all the same. But (your) life and (your) honor ... are more important than those of others, and so now you realize this just can't go on. ... The Party is making mistakes, many mistakes, grave ones. The consequences are clear, there's no concealing them, you can't just cover up hunger, cold, a lack of seeds, of draft animals, of tractors, you can't just cover up defeat. Is the party allowed to make mistakes, is it allowed to smirch itself with the filth of defeat? No, the Party must always be right. ... To purify, you need pure water, good soap (for example, you ...). The nominal reason a person dies for it is completely irrelevant."

"Did you figure that out there—in the northeast? So fast, before your twenty months were up?"

"Yes, that's dialectical."

Now the accused turns the accusation around, carrying the logic of Stalinism to its conclusion:

"And so those who have made mistakes in the name of the Party have to take the blame, to perish as counterrevolutionaries, so that the Party may remain blameless—stern, but just. I, too, have naturally made mistakes, I have to die. But if so, then let's do things in order! We'll start with your boss. His portraits hang everywhere, every single child in the tiniest village knows that everything happens according to his command ..."

"Enough, more than enough. You'll drop this reformist claptrap, you'll break, you'll admit to killing your own mother if that's what we want."

"We—who is we? Not you, you'll rot in the northeast (if you don't manage to bring me round)."

It all comes down to grasping the dizzying twists and turns by which the roles of perpetrator and victim switch places, the insane furor of the party apparatus that subjects every simple conflict between innocence and guilt to organizational deconstruction. The accused, the victim of an accusation that clearly and admittedly has nothing to do with him, is himself a perpetrator, has pronounced and carried out death sentences against comrades, not only, as he will say in his own defense, not only by sending them off to fight the enemy with transparent orders, trusting that his underlings will understand them, but also in the course of the struggle against internal opposition, for the purification of the party, with arguments identical or analogous to those he is now victim of. The prosecutor, as the accused rightly surmises, is himself a former exile, sent off under some pretext or other, certainly, at any rate, because the leadership deemed him suspect or dispensable. He comes out with the prospect of rehabilitation, with the offer to become a perpetrator himself, to send others off to the camps, but also with the threat of becoming a victim in his own trial if he comes up short. But the imperative of bringing the highest-ranking comrade, the peak of the hierarchy, into this hyperhierarchical movement of de- and rehierarchization, will not be fulfilled until his death in 1953. Still, even if all lines in a pyramidal organization converge in a precise point, a single body, and the paranoia of the head has structural effects on the entire body—and even if the process of de-Stalinization began at the precise moment of Stalin's death—we may still conclude that the logic of this organization will not change simply because one name substitutes another, even if the name in question is that of the organization itself (Stalinism). For in this institution, structured around the polarities trust/mistrust, loyalty/betrayal, paranoia is rooted not in a specific character but instead in a precise location on the vertical axis of the party's spectrum of power. The leadership's paranoia is the effect of the absolute certainty of the masses. The base's blind trust in its leadership constantly regenerates and reconfirms it. "When the writer Sholokhov criticized the cult of personality, Stalin replied with a smile: 'What can I do? The people need a god'" (Montefiore, 163).[3]

Crucial, because paradigmatic for the understanding of the logic of the party, is the argumentation of the prosecutor, which is more realistic as regards the specific reality of the party than it may appear; in this complex role-playing game, its cards are on the table, far more so than those of his opponent, who finds himself on the defensive. Like a good pedagogue, he demands that the person to be educated arrives at insight into the educational measures to be imposed on him; it just happens that the educational measure in question is a death sentence, which moreover bears no direct relation to the offenses for which the offender is to be punished. He should sacrifice himself for the party, which has chosen him for this sacrifice in order to avert damages to the party for which he is not answerable. Why, asks the helper, addressing the one in need of help, does he—he, who in other circumstances is ready to sacrifice himself to the party, and to sacrifice others to it, too, in the struggle against external enemies—why does he refuse to die now, when the party is looking for someone ready, just once, for one last time, to voluntarily play the guilty party?

Mauser, the only play by Heiner Müller (56) to be expressly forbidden in the German Democratic Republic (GDR), puts in evidence the Stalinist aspect of this party dialectic, and that of Brecht along with it.

The Revolution no longer needs you / It needs your death. But until you say Yes / to the No that is addressed to you / You have not yet done your work. / In front of the gun barrel of the revolution, which demands your death / Learn your last lesson. Your last lesson, which goes: / You, pressed up against the wall, are your enemy, and ours, too."

This logic is consistent. If the whole of the party is greater than the individuals who make up its parts, if the means of the communist revolution don't matter so long as it achieves its end, then the individual should not object to the shared goal and the means of reaching it merely because a requirement for its being reached is that she herself not reach it. She wants communism, therefore she wants the party, the party wants communism, therefore the party wants her, the party wants her death, therefore she wants to die. She wants to die, so concludes this logical conclusion, to the degree that she does not renounce her ideals, betray the party, betray communism.

What a chain of equivalencies, furor of representation, logic of identity. Lenin has literally made this point in the most blunt manner at the Eleventh Congress of the Russian Communist Party (Bolsheviks) (RCP[B]), literally because the dimensions of his analysis do not extend beyond a single point: "And the state is the workers, the most advanced part of the workers, the avant-garde, that is us" (Schritkopcher, 21). Even on the logical plane, this trope of identification not only violently cuts away everything from the party's members that steps out beyond the party line but also robs them of that surplus that the party should have extended to its members in accordance with its own promises. As an organization, it was supposed to lead individuals out of isolation, consigning them to a better future. But instead of pointing past the strictures of individualism, the party confines these individuals within the boundaries of a bounded generality. The communists, obsessed by the party, possessed by its mission, become its possession. The party promises to guide people away from private property relations, but the party itself cannot leave them behind.[4] Not only the means, but the all-too-terrestrial individuals, are subordinated to the end, the goal, this real-unreal transcendence. And yet ends-oriented rationalism, in the tension between means and ends, retains rationality and remains open to criticism based in rational criteria. If the end, being sacred, consecrates the means, then it is the light that renders the ugliness of the means visible.

A more refined investigation of the specific historical formation of this ends/means logic and the time structure that embeds it, that is embedded within it, is necessary to bring to a provisional conclusion an analysis of the party and its complicated, delayed dissolution. For ends/means logic sustains a specific relationship to time in which the present is only justified with view to a future it must strive constantly, single-mindedly to approximate. "So sublime is the revolution that it is enough to live for it, and the present becomes pale, hollow, if it does not serve as a preparation for the great upheaval" (Sperber, 115). A promised future, it promises not only salvation from the woes of capitalism but also compensation for the privations, lies, and toil its abolition demands. It promises to repay in one fell swoop all the guilt accumulated through the ruthless application of means. It is as if a credit had been taken out with thousands of creditors who daily renew and augment their commitment, their contribution, and every year they hope to see this credit redeemed, thousands of communist creditors and a single debtor, the party. Its rigid exclusivity, its unforgiving antagonism to any and all deviations, makes clear that only those who toe the line and remain faithful to the end may reckon on seeing any dividends. And at the same time—this is the insidious feedback loop, total risk sharing—the success of the enterprise depends entirely on those it employs, on the creditors themselves. Their failure results in an eternal deferment of dividends—no pain, no gain—and if these benefits grow ever more remote, that too is their fault alone. And yet the promise will continue to be held out, however improbable and unbelievable its fulfillment may become—until the day of its final insolvency (1990). What a disappointment when those betrayed must finally admit it was a deception; how much more so when they are forced to recognize they themselves are the deceivers.

To all appearances, the Communist Party functions according to a pattern far older than mere bourgeois models, borrows from religion, which must disburse consolation for the vale of tears of the present—and encourage work. But in its reified form, the party may be described as specific machinery of a capitalist type—cooperative, credit union, and factory all rolled into one—that applies its hierarchical organization, economic efficiency, and military discipline less to the production than to the advertising of one single product: the future, the communist future.

Yet this future never became present, nor did it remain future. Utopia lost: this strange, wispy phrase, which sounds rather like the title of a conference of theologians, means quite simply that today, the greater part of the future already lies behind us. This and this alone is the meaning of all talk of the end of history. It is the realization of the (Popperian) motto, which seems to have set the mood for the world after 1990: the world that has been vindicated may not be the best of all worlds, but it is the best of all worlds that exist. It is sympathetically sedate compared to the mindless white lies of Stalinist panegyrics. But right from the first, this slogan, which presents itself in the rhetoric of compromise as dispassionate coolheadedness, is beset with a dreadful sorrow. They have not stopped to linger because things are so nice but rather because they lack the courage to go on. Movement is pointless. This is what makes the jubilant cries of the Cold War victors so unconvincing: they lack all joy. Instead of relief at averting looming danger or shared joy at the newfound fortune of the former oppressed (Russia's newly minted millionaires?), it expresses something resembling embittered malevolence: the schadenfreude those who stayed home feel for their siblings drowned at sea. Victory is thus tarnished by foregoing defeat. The anticommunists didn't win, they capitulated to the immutability of fate. Anticommunists do not win, they give up: they give up their dreams. This is the origin of the cliché—those who aren't socialists when they are young have no heart, those who remain socialists when they grow up have no brain. Growing up: here, that is just another term for losing hope. Apologetics for the status quo are based not on the celebration of the true but on the restriction of mourning for the possible; not on fear for what has been achieved, but on fear of what is achievable. Both, however, have their basis in history. That is the rationale for this book.

Whoever doesn't want to talk about Stalinism had better keep quiet about communism. But what can be said about Stalinism by those who refuse to hear about communism? Those who wish to write the history of this past without writing about the history of that future that was buried in it? Just like relative value theory, the comparative analysis of domination always avoids the very thing it oscillates around eternally: domination itself. It can only be understood in light of its possible abolition, and this possibility, like all possibilities, exists subject to the peculiarity that its realization depends on its becoming real as a possibility: the possibility of freedom from domination does exist, but not a priori, only historically.

This is the advent of communism. Unlike the slaves, who only wished to be as free as their masters, unlike the peasants, who wanted to give the lords a tenth of their crop instead of a fifth, unlike the bourgeoisie, who only wanted political freedom, not economic freedom, what the workers demanded was a *classless society*. What the communists promised was the abrogation of all dominance. And as long as they are remembered, their promise remains. It is common for dominance to dress itself up as freedom, and these have been nearly the only garments it has donned since the bourgeois revolution, if not earlier; but ever since those who fought against all domination themselves rose to dominance, something has changed. And everyone who counts off all the roads paved with good intentions or pronounce, in resignation, that power has won out over all ideas ignores this something. *Man is born bad* is the many-faced formula in which this work of mourning concludes; a historical melancholy disguised as realism on the societal level. Many variations on the same sentence oppose it: most naively, *Man is born good*; most radically (biopolitically speaking), *Man is unborn.* But any riposte on the anthropological level fails to address the structure of dream and mourning by which *resignative realism* keeps denying its relationship to history. Man is the enemy of man, he has always slaughtered his own and will go on doing so in the future. War yesterday, war today, war tomorrow. That sounds dreadful—but it *is* far more dreadful than it sounds. For the assertion of the repetition of the same is actually a consolation that covers over the true horror. If it was always bad, then really nothing bad has happened, nor can anything really bad happen. To have learned everything from the past and therefore to be incapable of learning anything from the future, even when the only thing there was to learn was fear, is a pernicious consolation. A consolation that can no longer console, since a future has been promised in which the lessons of the past are no longer valid, in which there is no more cause for fear. Stalinism, this "crime against the future of mankind," is not just any dominance, not just one more form of dominance, but instead the first and paradigmatic link in an unbroken chain of disappointments that could only be so devastating because they were based on a hope unknown to earlier generations (Knaudt, 3).

That is why the first reproach against anticommunism must be that of downplaying the crimes of Stalinism. Not because an idea was murdered alongside the people in the gulags—how cynical—but because communism alone brought forth into the world the historically actionable demand to accept no disenfranchisement, to tolerate no more degradation. Since that time, even the slightest injustice grows greater, and the greatest pain hurts exponentially more.

4 Class

But if there is a sense of reality ... then there must also be something we can call a sense of possibility. ... So the sense of possibility could be defined outright as the ability to conceive of everything there might be just as well, and to attach no more importance to what is than to what is not.
—Robert Musil, *The Man without Qualities*

Class is dead. Even in a class society, it seems easy to write this. For there are—here, now—not many signs of life that can oppose this diagnosis in any meaningful way. Nor—perhaps—can any contemporary form of life rise above the thousand deaths that compel it to put forth such a verdict, to note it down soberly. There are more people living now than ever before in history. That isn't true for the communists. For them, a small minority of the living is faced with the overwhelming majority of the dead.

The defeat of class, its incapacity, often its unwillingness, to prevent National Socialism, makes it hard to argue against. At least in present-day Germany, it seems easy to bury the historical corpse of class, or easier still, to leave it lying on the side of some road we no longer take. It is hard to know whose loss we are failing to mourn, it is hard, almost impossible for us, the living, to know who was this body we are burying in an unmarked grave. We can only guess who this class of combatants was, those whose mission failed, who perished in violent disgrace. Heritors of unknown forebears, we stand in their shadows, because the sun of progress, which we are no longer willing to believe in, glows behind our back. The voices, here the voice of Weiss (54), echo up from their coffins, whisper about that break that was itself broken off, the first in the history of humanity, with an irrepressible resonance, to give language to those who had always been cut off from the word:

There was a time when we had furiously denied that the reading of a book, a visit to an art gallery, of a concert hall, of a theater would demand of us additional sweat and headache. Since then, attempts to escape speechlessness belonged to the functions of our existence, what we found in the process were first articulations, basic patterns from which to emerge from muteness and take measured steps into the cultural realm.

Steps into the cultural realm of the bourgeoisie, a realm made strange, made hostile. The language to be learned is the language of the others, the reigning language spoken by those who reign. To learn it means to make it one's own, to wrest it from its legitimate owners, to purloin and appropriate it, to twist it around until it is suitable for the articulation of one's own experience.

"Every word," Weiss (24) writes elsewhere about the period of the National Socialist underground, "had to be salvaged from powerlessness, in order to discover that tone ... in which we invested ourselves with endurance, confidence, and vital force." In order to find that tone that also, or at another time, is capable not so much of confirmation and consolation as of calling forth a sense of discomfort with the present, or making a silently existing discomfort oscillate, oscillate until it can be heard. The words one appropriates, the words appropriate to oneself, the words that correspond to one's own story, and in which they are uttered anew, can be spread, spread around, passed on. And they are passed on and taken up, ineptly, zealously, in the hunger for language. "It was," Glaser (40) writes, "as if I had spent years readying the place to record the words that I learned." This place is not empty, and if it is, then only in the sense that a blank in a text meant to be filled in is empty. At issue is not the primary expression of prelinguistic sensations of critique but instead of translation, transformation. Bourgeois language possesses concepts for equality, for justice, yet it hinders the articulation of capitalist exploitation, which is effected through the logic of free and equal exchange. The language of the proletariat—not the everyday communications of the working population, not a certain restricted code, but a political, politicizing language—elevates the experience of class to the plane of concepts and pushes it past the sighing of the workplace, the snarl of the laborer forced early out of bed, into the possibility of other experiences.

How liberating it was for me to hear terms that made of my vague aversion to the characteristics and customs of the old man a publicly recognized striving for the future and for the service of human happiness. [38]

The old man here refers ostensibly to the protagonist's old man, his father, an authoritarian postman who nearly beats his children to death, and at the same time, as petty bourgeois and later Nazi, is a metonym for the old itself, which passes down the tradition of domination that must be abolished.[1] The language of liberation is liberating because by putting a name to injustice, it abrogates its status as an unquestionable matter of course, and by making possible the communication of this injustice, it makes collectivity possible. If injustice is suffered collectively, it can be combated collectively. Class is formed through the language of the class struggle, and in it, through struggle, the possibility of the abolition of class becomes foreseeable. Now that *class* seems to have vanished, it is difficult to reconstruct the significance of this collective experience, and simply to cite the language it was articulated in, as a gesture of authenticity, is no longer possible. This language is too contaminated by its future, a future that is now past (a past which is a lot closer to our present), where it has congealed into dogmatism; it is a language that was silenced in an eternal present. The attempt to find a language open to the recurrence of an experience cast out of time cannot avoid the risk of pathos. For a language determined by the historical power relations that mold the present, the language of this hope and the language of its disappointment inevitably turn into an anachronism, a foreign language. At best, the experience of class can be approached from behind, working backward from the moment of its demise, in which that which has vanished still echoes painfully.

In the mid-1930s, the frozen language of the Communist leadership reads and sounds like this:

[He] no longer had his own language when it came to serious matters, only the supine, swaggering jargon of newspapers, which ... was like a symbol of impotence. ... In this conversation he had said, among other things: "The implementation of preparations for the revolution demands the implementation of the designation of the treasonous character of the SPD leadership." When he uttered this word, implementation, he banged his fist on the table, as if he had some sense of the feebleness of this, the only word that offered itself. (Sperber 162)

Sperber (162) remarks:

A leadership that has forgotten its verbs and can only express actions in abstract nouns inevitably paired to the word "implement" can neither pave the way for the revolution nor successfully unmask any treasonous character whatsoever.[2]

Nouns, which in German are moreover capitalized, like the names of institutions, symbolize the forsaking of offensives, of attacks, of revolution, in favor of retreat, defense, the Soviet Union; class huddled down behind the capital letters of its new fortress. Silence sets in, and with it a kind of realism. Description of reality as the affirmation of the extant and, presumably, the prohibition of the conditional: could, would, what if, if only vanish into the drawer labeled "deviations"—into suspicions of anarchism. This is a language that no longer promises. At the beginning of the thirties, this much is readily apparent.

Many good old comrades turned red with shame when a market crier encouraged people to join the party-affiliated labor unions and militias: "thirty, thirty-one, two, three, thirty-four—we still need another twenty-six to reach our goal—who's ready to step forward—who wants to do something more for his class—ahaaah, five, six, thirty-seven." (Glaser, 73)

The language of competition, of quantity, of accumulation, in which the figure of the masses, a mere number in the party book, prevails over the class (of consciousness). More and more, class's future disappears from its present, making way for the presence of tactical and economic calculus. And as the organization changes, so do the organized, a new type of party worker prevails. Glaser (73) continues:

The militant groups ... appeared at the gatherings with a marshal bearing, with stovepipe boots and iron heel taps clinking almost like spurs, with leather piping on their blue peaked caps. During the time of the general prohibition on uniforms the militias of all parties sidestepped the law by wearing purchasable caps, boots, and jodhpurs. Only from close up could you tell if those people clinking off in the distance were browns or people from our side. ... Comrades of ours showed these same affectations, but since they were the majority and they came closest to the taste of the "masses," and we had decided to become a party of the masses, the gatherings were more or less designed to rouse their enthusiasm.

And on the nights following the gatherings ... tired but riled up by the hours-long hunt—hunting the browns or being hunted by the greens—we walked bewildered through the dark alleys, each quieter than the next, four, three at a time ... aimlessly ... until morning. ... Our dream, the dream of young people taking pains to purify and prepare themselves—as though for a wedding—for their entry into the coming era, working relentlessly on themselves, terrified of bringing spiritual deficits, inhibitions, damage from the past into the future, like dirt on the soles of their shoes, seeking for and fighting over not only the path, but also the immediate and distant goal and the form the world should take: our dream grew remote, and we dreamt it with a guilty conscience.

No less strange than it is typical is this heterosexual metaphorics describing revolutionary desire: the traditional trope of matrimony that frames the relationship with the revolution, with the longed-for future. Revolutionary matrimony weds the victorious revolutionaries to a new, a better life. But until then, this life is not their bride but rather their fiancée. A fiancée promised through a contract between Father Stalin and Mother Party, on one side, and the future, on the other. The dowry consists of restraint, loyalty, daily work, and the future groom, the fiancé, is the one who provides it. At the very least. But is this description of the new militarism, of power posturing at the peak of the nationalist era, not resonant with the injury dealt out to decent and well-meaning workers, their feeling that they have been betrayed, cast aside by hypermasculine proles who are actually primping themselves for a completely different suitor, one they dress up for, whose tastes they aim to accommodate—namely, the masses? Just as one may describe the party in terms of both capitalist and religious machinery, here, at the moment when the language of class is transformed, we glimpse a political and a sexual—that is to say, heterosexual—economy.[3] Remote as these economies of desire may appear from the consistently antimetaphysical "worldview" of orthodox Marxism, still, they are both real and realistic. For as Glaser writes, the dream that they dreamt *became remote*, and only in *that* moment; in other words, it wasn't always so, it wasn't so before, it had once been *an earthly dream*. This image deserves respect and undivided attention, for it is this experience that, under altered power relations, can no longer be retraced; the experience of the real dream, of the presence of the future, derealized in the futureless presence of the end of history.

It appears in a surprising formulation in Glaser's book *Geheimnis und Gewalt* (Secret and violence), in an early passage toward which we now may work backward. This time, for a pleasant change, it is about the relationship between two women.

At times fifteen or more people might meet in Margaret's apartment, which was far from large. She was keen on seeing a constant stream of new faces, and every first-time visitor gave her the chance to point at the red plush daybed and discuss its historical significance. It had served "Rosa" as a resting place for the night whenever she had been in town. Margaret's eyes lit up as she recollected the old days, which seemed as far away to us young people as the birth of the redeemer. It stirred us, being contemporaries with a witness who had seen a person from "history" in the flesh.

"When I saw her for the first time," she mused before us, while we scrutinized her face, looking for a special glimmer left behind by the meeting with the great deceased. "Ach, that was right at the beginning, I said to myself, such a little woman, how can she do what she does with the market square all packed with people." She interrupted herself proudly: "Well, when you heard that Rosa was giving a speech, no worker stayed at home. And when she started talking—then I got it, it hit me straight in the heart." [Glaser, 61f.]

It is not so easy to read or transcribe this dream correctly, how easily, how much more easily now, we hear *mused to herself*. But it reads *mused before us*. Musing before. The dream is not some privatized beyond, an ineffable experience of the "dreamer" turned in on herself with vacant eyes, fleeing into a magic world she alone has access to, no, it is a shared, collective activity. Common invocation of the absent, which is a projection in a twofold sense: imagined and presented—that is, demonstrated. The demonstration of a dream. Romantic as these formulations may seem under present-day power relations, when even the wish, let alone its fulfillment, has become improbable, that is how unromantic they appeared to those who learned the language of class when it was still a spoken language—in contrast to the party Latin of later decades (cf. Adamczak a, b). We must try and ignore the film of guitars playing around the campfire that the objective historical process instinctively places before our eyes. Nothing in the scene quoted contradicts explicitly that to the contrary: its religio-Christian metaphorics draws the comparison into its orbit; still and all, what we see here is not nostalgic intoxication, a backward-facing longing shared by young and old through the transfiguring power of the old people's story. Despite all talk of a "history," which is placed in quotation marks—the past here is no more closed off from the present than the future—the struggle for which brings together the listeners with the storyteller and her story. Still—and this *still* arises only in hindsight, which knows things turned out differently—the revolution can be waged, the project Rosa Luxemburg began can be realized. Above all, though—and this is significant both for the question of nostalgia and for

that of mourning the departed: the death of the murdered revolutionaries can still be avenged. And it *will*
be avenged, for the revolution will come. No doubt exists, it is not a possibility but rather a necessity, and its
appearance is nearly at hand. The passage immediately
preceding the one cited, which takes place in the same
house just described, makes this clear:

> From time to time, one of those present would draw a vertical line
> on the wall along one of the picture frames, to which he would
> add the date. The line followed the inclination of the wall, while
> the picture continued to hang vertically. This game was repeated
> so often that next to the frame, there was a fan pointing down-
> ward, a precise indicator of the speed with which the building
> was sinking.
> We looked at it without concern. We compared the rotting
> dwelling with the old society and cheerfully followed the com-
> petition between the one's collapse and the natural law of
> maturing upheaval, which was surely the more powerful of the
> two. If someone had tried to warn us, we would have laughed off
> the doubter and mocked him as a fool, that's how unflappable
> our certainty was that our class's triumph would get us a new
> home long before the old one managed to bury us in its rubble.
> (Glaser, 61)

The natural law of upheaval, ripening, just around
the corner. The suspicion in the German workers' movement, still faithful to Kautsky's attentism, of the seri-
ousness of this idea, as to whether it is really meant to
signify a law decreeing economic collapse, is thoroughly
appropriate. Certainty that the communist future stands

just around the corner, that the unstoppable progress of natural laws governing society guarantee it, would then be to blame for the violent defeat of class, which could have been mitigated, even stopped, if only people had thought it possible. And certainly the deception of certainty, the assurance, trustingly, eternally repeated, that siding with the right class—and at times merely belonging to—meant they had made the right bet for the future in the right place and would, without a single doubt, be on the right side in the end, is responsible both for the throng of Germans who cherished victory above all else as well as for their sudden disappearance, for their embrace of their former enemies as soon as they took power. Concerning the rationale for the changing sides among the so-called casualties of March in 1933, the conservative antifascist Sebastian Haffner (133) soberly records:

A strangely German motif, this line of thought: "All Nazis' opponent predictions have failed to come true. They said the Nazis wouldn't win. Now they've won. This means their opponents were wrong. Therefore the Nazis are right." And then ... "Saint Marx, whom they always believed in, hasn't helped. Apparently Saint Hitler is stronger. So let's destroy Saint Marx's image on the altars and consecrate Saint Hitler. In our prayers, instead of Capitalism is to blame, let us say the Jews are to blame. Maybe that will save us."

The language of religion, which Haffner employs here polemically, is appropriate, for what we are looking at is clearly a question of faith, independently of how it is based on and justified through economic, political, or analytic terms. Faith. Wavering and unwavering. That same year, Sperber (201) has a communist say to her husband in a brief conspiratorial meeting:

Back then, twenty years before, you said just one more push and everything will be different. In the summer of '14 you said the working class would not allow a war. In the winter of '17, when you came out of the field hospital, you said: Now things are getting serious. Soon we'll be down to the last battle. In 1923 you repeated for weeks on end: Maybe today, maybe tomorrow, the terror will be over. Then you said this crisis is the last one, capitalism in Germany can't hold out any longer. And now you're saying the Party's on its way up and Hitler's going downhill. For twenty years you were wrong, you were always on the side that came out worst. ... For a long time now, I haven't had the strength to go on believing, to go on hoping.

The strength to believe. The strength to hope. In the historical moment when it becomes clear that faith in the revolution is a mere illusion serving only to hold at bay the long-overdue breakdown of the communist's threatened bodies, to get her through the days in hiding and the nights on the run, that it is an illusion she cannot sincerely believe in, a formula mechanically repeated to accompany rather than alleviate the person in need, then it is obvious the old saw about finding strength in faith is only half the truth. Wishing, wanting, and hoping demand strength too, often more than letting things be, giving up, or so it seems. This strength is not the psychic energy necessary to keep a lie alive once its expiration date has passed. It is the effort to resist, to resist the ever-stronger yearning to just let oneself go, to finally stop, to yield to circumstances, to the stream of events that drags one off into the depths. Where does this strength to hope come from, where is it drawn from, how is it granted, who receives it, and above all, when? For it is a question of time, not, or only barely, of spirit, of psyche, of character. A question of history, of the history of desire, of desired history. A question of historical conditions strong enough to grant the strength of a faith capable of looking past its history and therefore past the logic of faith itself. Not a faith, then, that eases resignation, that makes accommodation possible, not a counterfactual faith, but an antifactual one, a faith turned against reality, a faith inimical to, most likely even hostile to, reality. An antifaith that turns on itself with the same intensity as it turns on the conditions that gave rise to it. What conditions could grant the strength for such a faith? Are there any strong enough to free this faith from the history of faith?

Franz Jung writes how already, at the end of the twenties, the strength to hope has dried up among a small group of leftist deviationists, the Communist Workers' Party of Germany (KAPD), which at the time numbered forty thousand members. Their faith turned against itself, but in an utterly different way from that just theorized. The "hatred that lingers in the subsoil of every revolt, without which no revolt has no chance of erupting and being implemented," turns against the dream of revolution in a resigned and self-destructive manner.

> This hatred I encountered in the movement had changed targets. First it turned against the Party apparatus Moscow had instituted, against the surveillance system in simple theoretical discussions, against the infallibility principle Moscow's flunkies claimed for themselves, even if often, their "infallibility" only lasted a brief time. ... Rooted in the bitterness of growing disappointment, it turned against Moscow in general. ... In the end, it even turned against the Russian Revolution, which seemed already to have been betrayed ...
>
> Not a single hair—and this may be surprising—was touched on a Party official's head; none of the central bureaus were stormed, though doing so might have brought a bit of relief. ... The revolt turned against the attempt to change the prospect of the revolution, to prolong it ... against the party itself, the collapse of which was already in sight. This revolt didn't express itself violently, it smoldered under the pressure of deadly silence. People went home and tore up their party membership book. They stopped talking to each other and arguing in the factories. (Jung, 167)

This speechlessness emerges from mistrust regarding the language of class, the promises it has made above all. It is the refusal to go on speaking the language of the possible, which there is no strength left to consider possible after so many disappointments. At the same time, others, descendants for whom the revolutionary uprisings of 1918–1919 and the later failed attempts at a general strike are tales from another era that they never lived through, may have experiences of a totally different kind. A time of nonsimultaneity, which is the condition for a retreat into resignation and at the same time leaves the strength to hope intact. Measured against the number of party members of the SPD and the KPD, which says very little, a presumably revolutionary, at least potentially antifascist labor force still retains, in 1933, a possible hegemony, an improbable hegemony of the possible. The protagonist of Glaser's fictional autobiography relives in a few years a development that stretched on for several decades in the history of communism. As a vagrant who ran away from his small town in the twenties to escape from his authoritarian father, a later Nazi, he was picked up by the police and landed in a reformatory, met free-roaming nature enthusiasts (*Naturfreundejugend*), then anarchists, then communists; his experiences are suffused with ardent enthusiasm, with slightly secularized messianism. The experience of the future, a possible revolutionary future, is so present, so palpable, for him and for his comrades that on the day of their hire, their first bosses chase them off for demanding "all the conditions of all the labor unions" all at once (Glaser, 44). Glaser (42) writes about the appropriation of the communist history of nearly failed attempts at revolution:

I restlessly rounded out my knowledge. And the message came down to me from descriptions of the recent uprisings and revolutions that I belonged to a class charged with a unique, immense, eternal task, the salvation of mankind.

Not so much secularized messianism. Rather a missionarism, with a mission handed down by a superhuman superintendent (a task-charger), by a certain *history* that, in these formulations, is raised to the rank of a metasubjective subject. This messianic force—for it is a strong messianic force—is metaphysical, but it does not have to be. It needs no recourse to a superior power hovering over the fighters like an executioner's sword. Because it is not history that passes this historic mission down to the worker's movement, rather, this movement itself is already doing what it proclaims: making history itself. A human history, which is the history of those humans who set their own goals. That is the true, the unmetaphysical, the antimetaphysical core of this messianism without a messiah. Humans themselves are the forces of history, which they draw on as allies.

But the above formulation of the late twenties, which probably takes this form because historical power relations, the long line of defeats, objectively fuel the need for a powerful ally, for a metareal history of progress in contrast to the real history of impending catastrophe, already foretells the complicity of messianism with the failures and crimes of the party. What is completed in the formation of the party, a detached autonomization, has at least one of its origins here. A motif of reification: as soon as they recognize their power, the communists, who strip away the autonomy of human acts against humanity in order to slough off the incubus of the dead generations, grant it the autonomy to turn against them; estranged from themselves, they turn this power on themselves, bow down to it, which inspires confidence, to the sovereignty of the protecting leader whom they themselves have given the power to act through them and in their name. Swayed by the force of habit, they cede their power to the power of their own creation. It is evident that the oppression of the working class may be the work of the working class itself. What will deliver them—so they believe—is a savior on high. God—king—state—history—party.

This messianism, which is not messianism as such but rather *a* messianism, a certain messianism, is a messianism twice over. Its involvement is twofold. On the one hand, "this messianically contoured promise of another time, a new man, a happier society [leads one] ... to hold fast to the party and refrain from criticism, even as political developments clearly point in an authoritarian direction" (Diefenbach, 35). On the other hand, this messianic promise will show up the hollowness, the weakness of the communist movement quite early visible, later terminating in the petty bourgeois colorlessness of the German Democratic Republic. But the resistance this sensitization evokes is weak; all too quickly messianism allows itself to be once more confined to the private sphere, from which, in its religious form, it hardly dares to emerge. "Certainly," writes Glaser (62) about this messianism he has so impressively described, "no one would acknowledge it, because the model of a fighter we tried to emulate—all the parties had come up with their own model, their propaganda often showed pictures of them—was strictly law-abiding, hostile to flights of fancy, dedicated to stamping out petty-bourgeois sentimentality."

The critique of religion, the critique of metaphysics would mean placing all human production into the service of humanity, of human life. At the point that the motto *Die for the revolution, sacrifice yourself for Communism* can be considered rational, a reversal, a conversion is painfully evident. But the criterion that should help differentiate revolutionary actions from reactionary, counterrevolutionary ones cannot be clearly determined. Historical conditions exist that destabilize the borders between them. Like torture, employed to coerce the communists into revealing their comrades' hiding places. Shouldn't no one be able to resist it, let alone want to resist it, if it threatens to harm them, if it threatens their life? Or partisan warfare. If the fascist powers take hostage entire villages where partisans had been to supply themselves with necessary foods and medicines and then exterminate their inhabitants—as punishment, as a deterrent—should this not compel the antifascist resistance to give up, then and there? The compassion of the revolutionaries has its designated place in the strategy of those in power, who do not have freedom to gain but instead dominion to lose. If the good nature of the good is a fixed quantity of counterrevolutionary calculus, what else remains but to remain coercible? Which is not the same thing as allowing yourself to be coerced.

5 Promise

Beyond the acts of people [that] were actually carried out, there are those that could have been. These last are just as dependent on the times as the first, and they, like the others, have a history of their own, which shows their connections across many eras.
—Bertolt Brecht, *Große kommentierte Berliner und Frankfurter Ausgabe*

In 1927—just ten years after the October Revolution— Walter Benjamin (47, 66) summarizes his two-month stay in the city where people, though there are more many watchmakers than in any other, "do not get particularly worried about time," in this "most silent of great cities."

Moscow, as it appears at the present, reveals a full range of possibilities in schematic form: above all, the possibility that the Revolution might fail or succeed. (ibid., 132)

But is there a moment that reveals all possibilities? Brief as it may be, can a moment exist in which all possibilities are brought together, waiting to be chosen—for instance, on the streets of Moscow? And how many (of all) of the possibilities of success for the revolution are still recognizable in January 1927, how many have withered into unrecognizability, impossibility? Trotsky and Zinoviev are not yet banished from the party (November 1927), Zinoviev is still purging the Leningrad party (January–February 1926). The persecuted opposition is not yet being shot; so far it is only being imprisoned and exiled. "Members of the opposition removed from important positions. And in identical fashion: countless Jews removed from middle-level posts," Benjamin (11) notes soberly. And further on: "An attempt is being made to arrest the dynamic of revolutionary progress in the life of the state—one has entered, like it or not, a period of restoration" (ibid., 53).

How many possibilities for the success of revolution are discernible in a city where "one of the most conspicuous symptoms of the thoroughgoing politicization of life" is a "general atmosphere of cautiousness when it comes to openly revealing one's opinions" (ibid., 71, 33)? How many possibilities for successful revolution are apparent in a state in which the stores encourage the workers and peasants to unite with "hammer and sickle ... absurdly, executed in velvet-covered cardboard" (ibid., 27)? What perspectives for a classless society still exist in a society that, as Benjamin (9) remarks on the second page of his diary, ten years after the revolution—and this is true all the way to the end, and can still be seen by travelers today—is not even capable of getting rid of first- and second-class compartments on its trains?

How far back must one step in postrevolutionary history to pass the point where the possibilities of the revolution's failure start to outweigh those of its success, that counterrevolutionary "situation that makes all turning back impossible" (Marx a, 118)?

To pick up the thread, the faded, filthy red thread, to untangle it and roll it up, to follow it back through this labyrinth with its many twists and turns, all the way to the place where the path clearly divides into right and wrong, into exit and dead-end for the first time; to the place where failure lies buried, where errancy begins; to follow the path back to the point where one could have kept things from going this far, history from going this far: to here, to the place we are now. That is the phantasm, one of many, that motivates this book, that gives it its structure. As if there were a moment when that initial leap occurred in that which was formerly whole, as if this primal leap existed—and not a thousand leaps, a multitude of wounds, each a last one for those who leaped, and who were torn to pieces when they did so.

In history, in this history of the Russian Revolution, it is, it appears, always too late, too late for salvation. And yet the butcher Stalin, even after the destruction of the Communist Party, even after the disintegration of the Red Army, did not have to sign the pact with Hitler, could have formulaically announced his neutrality, could have readied himself for the coming war. The Social Democrats could have remained true to internationalism in 1914, the workers could have broken with the Social Democrats in 1918, they could have cooperated with them in 1933, if this was what the latter, the followers of Friedrich Ebert—mentor of the bloodhound Gustav Noske, leader of the Freikorps, the later SA—had wanted, which was not the case because they were already thinking in totalitarian-theoretical terms, with the historically victorious formula "Nazis = Kozis" (Wirtz, 43). The first three steps taken in seven-year boots through the history of the German workers' movement ends in a dilemma: Who is this all-too-knowing call addressed to, who is meant to heed the warning, receive the instructions, when no one cares to listen? And what if they did? What if they had heard, if they had ended, in other words prevented, the Nazis' seizure of power in the immediate aftermath of World War I with an, as it were, preemptive revolution? There would have been no Second World War, no war of annihilation, no Auschwitz. This remains true. From the antifascist perspective, the facts are clear: the question of anti-Nazism would not even have come up. But the communist question remains, the question of revolution. The face of Russia would have changed, its features would have relaxed: no longer hemmed in by enemies, receiving the large-scale economic aid that it required, it would have managed to ward off the shocking grimace of the lord of hunger. "The revolution may come earlier than we wish. Nothing is worse than revolutionaries having to worry about bread," Marx wrote to Engels in 1852 (Schritkopcher, 39). But what mask would it have worn, in this case? That of the underdeveloped child huddled in the handcart, dawdling behind the new-old German trailblazer? Could the socialist Germans in 1918 have broken the habit of trying to raise themselves above others, above all others? Or would a Russian campaign have followed a German revolution through other means, with one vanguard relieving the other?

"The science of history is the only science we know," Marx and Engels (a, 18) write in 1846, and yet they do not know the history that should have been their history, the history to come, the history bound to their thinking, later to their names, then finally just to their heads, hewed gigantic in stone, barricades against the future. The failure of struggles for the future in the past affects not only the present but also the relationships between these temporalities. The future today cannot simply be located in the moments of the present that point beyond it—there is no latent communism, no new society slumbering within the old—but instead must first be dislodged from the moments of the past in which they are anchored. Lines broken off. In the gaps between the compulsory historical context exist vanishing points whose vectors point in other directions.

Glaser tells in *Geheimnis und Gewalt* of an intellectual who looks for a similar thing under fundamentally
different historical conditions. He is an organic intellectual, sitting half starved in his study, fed by his comrades, the workers, in whose house he has found shelter:

> Rarely did he share the ten large leather suitcases that held his
> collection of all the summons, pamphlets, posters, and newspa-
> pers of the workers' movement from its earliest beginnings to the
> present time, preserved and arranged in stiff binders labeled in
> a tidy hand. Holding my breath, reverent and solemn as if stand-
> ing before the rediscovered correspondence of lost ancestors, I
> read the writings of the men from the conspiracy of equals, who
> wrote them before falling at the barricades in Baden or in Paris,
> being decapitated in the name of some sinister justice, vanish-
> ing into the wilderness, or dying in the misery of exile. I saw the
> membership cards of the Communist League, where the words
> "All men are brothers" were printed in twenty languages. Who was
> the stranger who had saved the stirring appeals from the Paris
> Commune, from the first zealous summons and the determined
> ordinances down to the last despairing entreaties, from annihila-
> tion? They had yellowed in their hiding place, but just as shadows
> still greet the living on the walls of convents, so they preserved
> the sound of struggle, the scent of gunpowder and blood, and the
> whiff of a dream of freedom and justice. (Glaser, 66)

The lost, murdered comrades are absent in a particular way, because the lines they followed are broken
off, because they had too little to bequest, and hardly
anybody cared or cares to inherit it. Unlike their victorious enemies in various parties—for they had many

enemies, and many were victorious, some (like fascism) more so than others—they were incapable of materializing themselves in lasting, visible traces, of institutionalizing themselves in architecture, laws, customs, thought patterns, manners of speaking. They are only—almost only—present as absences. In brief: they are gone. And their absence comes painfully into the consciousness of those who sense it, who dare to add to the discomfort of the present by asking which inheritance we could have accepted, what our departure point might have been had these communists survived, just a bit longer, just a bit more successfully. The past would be a different one and with it the present, palpably, perhaps a little, maybe even significantly.

If the word "if" wasn't there. That is the declaration of surrender. There is no other option than to surrender to this sad reality, because it has been robbed of any other possibility. This does not change even if the realist imperative ("Be Obedient") regarding the extant is formulated with the intention of being able to change. Thus one may well know how to change it, but not why, not into what. In the end, the injunction against imagining the possible exposes its speculative prudery in the final words of the German catchphrase cited in part above. The imaginable, which may not be imagined, stops short of the future, barely even reaches its own present. The monetary patriarchy, that's all there is to it—*My father would be a millionaire.*

But the conditions determining the possibility of possibility itself lie not primarily on the ideological but rather on the historical plane. And they improve—this is the thesis underlying the present investigation—the closer we come to the event of the revolution—this attempt to do *the impossible* (in the words of Che Guevara).

Nineteen twenty-two. Moscow.

In the square, nothing remains but the paving stones; no trees, no grass, nothing to be seen but the remains of the old fencing; the benches had long since been burned for firewood, holes gaped open where their iron legs had once been cemented inside—the iron was gone now, too, put to another use.

[He] came to this square with a dozen or so comrades employed, like him, in the commercial sector. They sat in a circle on the paving stones. They spread out their one meal for the day, which the office supplied them with: a bowl of millet porridge, baked to a thick crust, so you had to cut it off in pieces with a knife, and a cake of artificial honey, just as hard. That was it for the day. It was not only their shared midday meal, but at the same time their daily ritual.

During this pause from work, all of them could give themselves over fully to their dreams. They spoke together of the new Russia, of the great and powerful Soviet Union, which would soon rule over the world. As millennia of written history remind us, dreams are incomparably stronger than reality. (Jung, 150)

Let us linger a bit on this square in Moscow, not so much paved as strewn with stones, as Jung visualizes it. Let us take our place here, in this loose circle, let us allow this square to take hold of us and attentively record the effect. The pendulum of feelings, which swings in different directions, from nostalgic euphoria to righteous indignation, measures the distance, the historical gap between the scene as described and its invocation in the present. It reflects the struggles carried out since, victorious confrontations with orthodoxy and defeats at the hands of the bourgeois order; in rapid alternation, rise up that are closer and yet hardly present; we come to recognize the place we left behind to arrive here, to Moscow—Western Marxism, antiauthoritarian protest, queer feminism, the perverse politics of mourning (cf. Maak and Klingenberg). It is too quick, too easy—even if necessary—to hand out bad grades in ideology (sexist, racist, anti-Semitic) in accordance with the list of present-day communism's demands. The key is instead to salvage something that had been desirable among other power arrangements and is now sealed off in manifold ways. Something to catch hold of, something catapulted out into history with tremendous force by the revolution's explosion, like that manifesto of the Biocosmists from 1922 that demanded the "right to being (immortality, resurrection, rejuvenation) and to freedom of movement in cosmic space," because—as Fedorov had already argued—only the resurrection of the communist dead can cancel out the exploitation of the past by the future, in which those who struggled their whole lives long for communism themselves no longer benefit from it (Groys and Hagemeister, 14, 10).

It is a long road, and we walk it in fast-forward—even longer than the one taken by Jung, delegate of the KAPD, who was sent to negotiate with Lenin concerning admission into the Communist International and smuggled his way into Russia as a stowaway in a trunk below deck on a hijacked ship, traveled for days in trains on bombed-out routes, traces of the previous war of English aggression. As we sit down, the sun, which was blazing just a moment ago, has set. It is dark in the square, and only slowly, vaguely do the silhouettes of the people stand back up, those who had been here talking and who—let us not forget—had been eating too. The goal is to make the dead speak, but tentatively, without resorting to the trickery of the carny in the marketplace, the ghost speaker who puts words into their mouths. To make their dreams audible even when no one wants to hear them, even when these dreams are over—fulfilled, unfulfilled, and a strange combination of both. Dreams that, as it says here, in accordance with a millennial tradition, *for thousands of years have been incomparably stronger than reality*. They are so because, being based in reality, they may replace it by coming true. When we stretch out our hand, we can grasp the dreams still floating over the dust, unobserved by the passersby, the scant tourists scurrying over the pavement today:

In the circle I heard ... for the first time of the then still fanciful sounding plans for opening up and settling the uninhabited steppes between the Urals and Lake Baikal all the way to the Mongolian-Chinese border. In the middle of all the debates about the fine points of implementation stood man: not as a being that had created a god, had used this god as the foundation of a society, and had struggled to emulate this god, but rather man as material, as cornerstone, as cipher, as an intervention in the mechanics of existence. It may always be the individual who dreams, but the end effect and the goal erase the concept of the individual. ...

As for freedom and brotherhood, welfare for all and other such phrases ... problems that would be best solved after the agricultural ones, fertilizer, irrigation, soil chemistry, air and sunlight ...

If this Soviet economic center, which was to replace Europe, were to be built by means of capital flows—the North American continent was built up under similar conditions three hundred years before, along with the importation of slaves and outcasts—all the capital in the world today would not suffice. In the new order of consciousness, mankind is the better instrument ...

We argued about all this ten years before the deportation of the peasants from Ukraine, twenty years before the Chinese Revolution. We were staking out perspectives as we intuited or understood them. Based on the thought-paths of Charles Fourier, which Lenin had employed in sketching out guidelines for us: the Great Initiative; in terms appropriate to contemporary China: the Great Leap Forward.

We argued about all this. Blazing sun on the square, no trees, no bushes, not the least trace of green. Only a few people were walking across the square, no one to speak of. All over, groups sat on the paving stones, employees of government offices, spreading out their midday meal—the elite of the growing Soviet apparatus, demobilized Red Army soldiers, former students and workers and farmers who were trained for political-administrative posts during the years of the war between white and red.

No speakers riling up the masses, no fanatical zealots. Dreamers in a distant future, a future brought nearer with every workday, with every sunny day, with the hunger that enveloped and sustained them. The sun burned terribly on the square. (Jung, 154)

Not even with slaves would such a transformation be possible, Jung remembers people arguing a half century before. In fact, it will be slaves, forced laborers, who achieve this miracle and others like it. They will be harnessed to the enormous project of compensatory capitalization of the vast statist machinery that began, irrespective of the New Economic Policy, to link up with other momenta of capitalist production, with the still remaining monetary flows. A statist machinery demanding forced labor as a rational economic consideration, which will lead the assorted secret services and political police to compete for the highest arrest quotas (cf. Armanski, 153). Jung will know this in 1960, when he writes his memoirs. But he refuses to comment from the future, lets the original voices emerge scratchily from the literary gramophone. Suspicious, perhaps, of the progress of knowledge, he keeps himself from intervening in an all-too-knowing manner, from cutting himself short, from cutting his dreams short—the dreams he was able to dream back then, and later will no longer be able to dream. And yet he fails to bring the old voices to life: his utterances as autobiographer, as actor playing himself, emerge in a raspy tone. "I lived this immense power," Jung (256) writes, and yet he no longer manages to convey it; with this flat tone of resignation in his voice, it is hard to believe he (as opposed to Glaser) had once been capable of hope. And yet he works, slogs, strains, as if only a style as sober, as dispassionate as possible permitted him to portray those *dreamers in a faraway future* who were less dreamers than dream workers, workers on a socialist dream. All ornamentation must be cleared from the plain stage of this dream, there are no passersby, no one is out for a leisurely stroll, *no one to speak of*, and above all *not the least trace of green*. No picturesque mood, no atmospheric metaphors of hope sprouting up as in springtime. Just human cogwheels sweating from the strain amid the heat in a rather Fordist machine of desire.

Arriving here from history, working backward, we may try to engage in a spectral conversation with the dead. Feeling our way haltingly toward the moments of hope, which can only be salvaged truthfully through history, not by dispensing with it. Hence this construction, which begins at the end. Hence this procedure of antihistoric historiography, which is not antihistoric in the sense of opposing a given concept of history but instead opposes history itself. Which does not, like genealogy, turn to the past to make the present comprehensible but rather tries to grasp its unfulfilled future, a possible present that never managed to become *the* present. Its task is not to strip present reality of its natural armor, not to pay tribute to the tributaries, the thawed runoff, of history, not to reveal the matter-of-fact as a matter-of-acts, as the matter that composes the factual. Rather to breathe into the dust of history, make it whirl, so that in it, as in an animated film, the phantoms of a possible future will become visible.

Hence this tentative way of proceeding, hence the extension of history via fictional graphics, subjunctive instruments whose utility depends on how far they succeed in imposing their historically inappropriate transparencies over the image of history as given. It attempts to render realistic an impossible possibility, an unrealized potential, in order—perhaps—to realize it. But when it envisions it, when it *dreams it up*, it is not sleepwalking, and even if, at times, it dances in dreams, it doesn't lose itself among the clouds in the sky, doesn't search for a pristine origin point where history can be lifted off its hinges. Just as reality is spectral for it, densely packed with the presence of absent specters of possibilities suppressed, so too are the specters real, rising up from reality, operative in reality, laden with curses of all kind. This does not mean in the least that there is cause for retrospective joyous anticipation.

So it is with the outlines of these specters from Moscow, which are slowly filling in. Already evident in their indistinct forms, in the blighted glow of the dream of the New Man, in man as material, in the materialistic disenchantment of the Enlightenment heaven, is his devaluation into pure labor capacity, the reduction of the communists to mere matter, of worker to machine, which postcapitalist society iterates. Demystification renounces the lie of a certain inviolable human dignity, which bourgeois ideology conjured up for man in order to console him for the degradation of his everyday life, and along with it, renounces the claims it entails. A dream, then, whose resurrection is barred by its fulfillment. Can we follow the gaze of Communists into a future that today is already past, especially as it has been forgotten? Into a future that is capable, that would have been capable, of breaking free of the repetition of the same, of the presence of the ever-same victorious past.

Power had always overcome the masses for the simple reason that it was power. And the masses shouted "hurrah" and "long live," they sang, roared, killed, were killed, and sank off into namelessness. That was a story old as death. If the masses ever took power, ever held onto it—then power would lose its name and its essence, and the masses their namelessness, their lack of humanity. (Sperber, 423)

If—only! But thinking of wishes is not the same as wishful thinking, for reality draws sustenance from dreams. The promise persists because it is unredeemed. Hence it can be gathered and injected into a desire capable of resisting the temptation of realist capitulation. Communist desire, which will no longer permit itself to be tamed through anticipatory obedience to a certain reality.

The rubble of history obscures the view of the dream of it, but not entirely: there are gaps through which glints of the dream of the once possible future, later made impossible, appear. This is true anywhere the past does not conceal the past future, where the later image of the history that arrived does not mask the earlier image of the history to come. Awkward, damaged, ashamed, it peers out, it would just as soon hide behind later events for which it—rightly—feels responsible. And yet there are these splinters—with cracked, dirty, rough, impure edges, splinters of a power now past that history has not managed to bury. They can be used to write messages, to carve memories into the skin, tattoos that can easily fade and will often need to be touched up.

And so if, along with the specters from this Moscow square—likely long buried under new asphalt—we turn our gaze toward a past future, we will not see history, the past, or the impending past of a certain present, but instead: a future. Not—and this is critical—pure future, not the pristine image of a pure world, but rather the image of a world to come, under millions of layers, surrounded by menacing images of the past. These images, these old maps of a possible future are legion, and their number is growing. At times they are indistinguishable from the future sought, from the very land being sought. And therein lies the trick: only the wrong maps can point out the right way.

Except there is no trick, no metaphysical grasp capable of bending past defeats into signposts toward a future victory. No narrative of progress that can free an unreal dream from the violent embrace of its history in which it became a nightmare. Those who died in the Stalinist terror died in vain. Jung (120) offers a sober rejection to all hopes for a materialist sublation:

The workers' movement [follows] statist laws that Karl Marx characterized more clearly than in his analyses elsewhere with the words: The workers' movement can only learn from defeats—reason enough for the party's theoreticians to follow to wait, primarily and almost exclusively, for defeats to occur.

At least in this connection, the theoreticians to follow and those who did follow, the theoreticians of partisanism without a party (cf. Karschnia, 296ff.) have an advantage over their predecessors; they no longer have to wait on defeats—there are more than enough already. But who among them today is willing to make these defeats their own, who is willing to step into a tradition that every reasonable leftist wants to have broken with always already? Who is willing still today to write herself into a history that the former Stalinists and New Philosophers with their "cult of personality" and their *Black Book* wrote themselves out of as dubiously as they did despairingly?[1] Who will let herself be persuaded to accept a bequest consisting above all of debts, of guilt?

Who, today, would dare to learn from the defeat of the Russian Revolution? And from which defeat?

Into the mid-1970's, the "Russian question" and its implications was the inescapable "paradigm" of political perspectives on the left, in Europe and the U.S., and yet 15 years later seems like such ancient history. This was a political milieu where the minute study of the month-to-month history of the Russian revolution and the Comintern from 1917 to 1928 seemed the key to the universe as a whole. If someone said they believed that the Russian Revolution had been defeated in 1919, 1921, 1923, 1927, or 1936, or 1953, one had a pretty good sense of what they would think on just about every other political question in the world: the nature of the Soviet Union, of China, the nature of the world CPs, the nature of Social Democracy, the nature of trade unions, the United Front, the Popular Front, national liberation movements, aesthetics and philosophy, the relationship of party and class, the significance of soviets and workers' councils, and whether Luxemburg or Bukharin was right about imperialism. (Goldner)

That is the trail this text is following, from one defeat to the next defeat, from one ending of the Russian Revolution to the next. Endless endings. But it is a trail that the text is trying to pick up from where it had broken off. "Not more history, but prehistory," Loren Goldner writes. As if the presence of the end of history were as distant from the past of communist history as both of them together are from the communist future, the end of prehistory. What temporal distance. More than a temporal distance in a time out of joint. Today it is not only the revolution that has been lost, but even more so, its defeat. The loss of loss. What does such a defeat still have to teach us? And how? What can a defeat teach us when it is no longer suffered from? How is one to mourn it? These questions open on to further questions, fundamental questions. If the history of the revolution can only be written as or through the history of its defeat, then how shall we write this history if—a terrible suspicion—there was no victory to precede it? If the history of its end were actually the history of an end without end, of an end without a beginning, of a parting without an arrival?

A loss may only be mourned through the memory of that which was lost. That which was, that which happened. "The memory of something that did not happen is an impossible memory" (Loick b, 60). How then should one mourn a thing that can't be remembered, that never was? How, save through a dream of something that could have come true. Mourning and dreaming: since mourning does not come without dreaming, dreaming no longer comes without mourning. For the possible is not simply an idealistic opposition to the real, its preconditions are rooted in the historical struggles. Hence it is necessary to work backward toward historical phases when the conditions for the possible were better. But today there is no dream of another world, be it a utopian image or an atopic prohibition of the image, that the nightmares of limbo, of the transitional phase, do not obscure. If we do not engage with the history of attempts at revolution there will be no more desire for revolution. Mourning, dreams, and trauma, the third enveloping the second, the first the only possible means of prying the third apart. What weighs on the possibility of communist desire is not just the end of history but first and foremost, the end of the revolution. Not just 1989, but even more so, 1939, 1938, and so on back to 1924, to 1917.

6 Revolution

We had practiced and preached hatred of the circumstances
of our existence; needlessness was our greatest enemy.
—Georg Glaser, *Geheimnis und Gewalt*

In 1924, on January 27, to be exact, the Russian Revolution's coffin is carried to its gravesite. On the shoulders of Stalin and—still—Zinoviev, both in front, leading this immense funeral march. Carried to its gravesite, but not buried, instead preserved to be observed in a palace hastily erected at thirty below zero, in a gray wood hut in the middle of Red Square. In the center of the coffin, carefully sheltered from the weather and accompanied by a thousand Communists, like the body of the revolution itself, is the corpse of the great revolutionary, whose name is posted in large letters on this first, provisional mausoleum: LENIN. Immortal victim of a more or less natural death, whose mortal body already bears the first signs of decay. The skin is turning brownish, the entire body splotched with spots the color of parchment, the lips already retracted one millimeter apart (Zbarsky and Hutchinson, 7).

At end of October 1923, before Lenin's death, a secret meeting of the politburo, following a suggestion
by Stalin, had passed the resolution to preserve Lenin's
body. Trotsky was opposed: "If I have understood Comrade Stalin correctly, he is suggesting replacement of
the relics of Saint Sergius of Radonezh and Saint Ser-
aphim of Sarov with the relics of Vladimir Ilyitch (ibid.,
7). Bucharin too sees in the embalmment a "notable
whiff of clericalism" of a kind Lenin himself would denounce, and suggests as an alternative honoring Lenin's
memory by reprinting his writings in editions of a million copies and changing the name of Petrograd, the
capital of the revolution, to Leningrad (ibid.). All these
suggestions will be taken up, there will even be Lenin
Hills and a yearly holiday to commemorate his death,
when all the entertainment spots must close (Benjamin,
149, 111). In the center of this culture of remembrance,
which is really more of a culture of contemporization,
of dehistoricization, or in its own words, a culture "of
the perpetuation of Lenin's memory," the mausoleum
is unmissable. The "totally botched Lenin mausoleum,"
as Benjamin describes it three years later, when he sees
the wooden building, before the crumbling materials
are replaced with red and white granite. As if a mausoleum for the mummification of a communist revolutionary could somehow be successful. If only, Benjamin
perhaps thought, it weren't *crowned* with a portico, if
only it hadn't been shaped like a six-tiered *pyramid*. If only

the coarse plaster statue of a worker, in memory of the fighters in the October Revolution, had not been pulled down, because the structure commemorating the leader of the October Revolution disturbed the *symmetry* of Red Square. In this panorama, framed by the venerable czarist Kremlin complex, all architecture seems to have congealed into allegory. Against it, flags are faded and no longer flutter in the icy cold. The crossed hammer and sickle on the red background are going gray. They will never have come to stand for anything in the nation of workers and peasants, which will never become a workers' state, certainly not a peasants' state, but only ever a state, period. The Lenin mausoleum is, beyond compare, *the* symbol of the Russian Revolution.

And what a symbol it is. Lenin, resting on his back, eyes closed, hands placed irreligiously by his hips. Instinctively the visitor walks on her tiptoes to keep from waking him from his sleep. Lenin, in his greatcoat and pants, their dull khaki color recalling his soldier days and harmonizing beautifully with the color of his overly made-up skin, with a yellow tinge that brings to mind the acrid scent of rot that permeated him in the days immediately following his death. Beneath his uniform, which is laced in the back, the revolutionary leader's body is wrapped in elastic bands splashed from time to time with a salve that keeps the corpse moist. To prevent their sinking, his eyes are replaced with prostheses, the lids sewn shut, the lips sealed with sutures concealed beneath his mustache. For the first time in history, a mummy lies not under bandages, but visible in an open coffin. Conserved for terrestrial eternity through a ritual bath performed every eighteen months, in 240 liters of glycerin, 110 kilograms of potassium acetate, 150 liters of water, and 1 to 2 percent chloroquine (Zbarsky and Hutchinson, 29). The sight of this living corpse stuns even Nadezhda Krupskaya, Lenin's widow, who was always opposed to the "external worship of Vladimir Ilyich's personality," to the erection of "monuments and palaces in his name." While she grew increasingly older, Lenin enjoyed eternal youth (ibid., 5, 36).

To take hold of his legacy, whether solely to perpetuate it or cut off all possibility of its perpetuation, we must know where the dead body lies buried, as the hauntologist, the specter-teacher Derrida teaches. To stop him from returning uncontrolled, from multiplying and changing form, to take possession of his spirit, to turn it into intellectual property, we must know the exact place where we can identify the deceased and exorcize his unwelcome specter. We needn't worry that grave robbers have stolen the remains, that worms have eaten them, that they have rotted to nothing, for in Lenin's case, the place is well known. He lies at 5° 45'13" north, 37° 37'11" east, visible to all the world, seen by all the world, scientists, pilgrims, tourists. With just one interruption—from 1941 to 1945, when the German Wehrmacht's approach required an armored transfer to

Tyumen in western Siberia—he has lain there, from the time of his death down to today. Lenin, still, bathed in pale light, is not exactly peppy or vivacious; he seems rather to be sleeping softly, not dead, but undead. Lenin, the undead. Neither present nor absent, neither dead nor living, neither body nor spirit. Even if his brain has been carefully removed and placed in a special case to be marveled at in an institute founded for the purpose of studying his genius (Hagemeister, 36), it is certainly more than a mere body, a material, lifeless thing that lies here, housed in the mausoleum.

"When, as assistant to Professor Vorobyov and my father, I set foot in the mausoleum for the first time," writes Ilya Zbarsky, who, like his father, will devote his own life to artificially extending Lenin's, "I was overwhelmed by the place's solemnity. In the middle of a room dense with shadows, I saw Lenin's catafalque. The imposing sculpted bronze consisted of a lower part in the shape of hanging flags, and a cone-like cover. Inside, the thin bundle of whitish lights converged on the face and hands of the dead. As we took our place around the coffin, I heard the sound of an electric pulley. Slowly the glass lid rose up from the four corners of the catafalque, where it had rested on a kind of piston mechanism" (Zbarsky and Hutchinson, 28).

An overwhelming sensory experience, no doubt, not just sensory, but—and who could not feel this?—supersensory. And yet the patriarch of the Russian

Orthodox Church, Alexy II, is wrong when he explains in 1993 that Lenin's "wicked soul" will continue to "hover over Russia" until he is buried (ibid., 46ff.). By then, the mausoleum laboratory has already begun preserving the bodies of Russian mafia bosses, who are honored in their monuments in Adidas tracksuits, "no longer embalming political leaders, but rather the masters of the economy" (ibid., 51). The priest, the ghost hunter Alexy II is wrong, Lenin's spirit haunts nothing. He has not returned, unforeseeably, unexpectedly, has not multiplied into countless avatars. He is not, following the hauntologist Derrida's (xx) definition of the spirit as undefinable, "more than one." Lenin's specter is not irreducible, but reduced, because canonized, into one: the spirit—of Leninism. A spectral identification. Leninism, that is itself a Stalinist term, a term invented by Stalin, Leninism is Stalinism. The domestication of the *per definitionem* undomesticable—that is what these materialists have achieved. The spirits they called respond to the names given them, and if they dare to articulate themselves in the service of rebellion as a different, authentic, insurrectionary Lenin, the mausoleum's overseers will dispense with them once more. With the Red Army's help if necessary. A specter then, *a* spirit of Leninism, but a specter that does not haunt, that is instead told when to come and go by the party leaders standing on the mausoleum's platform waving to the passing processions mourning and paying their respects. As if these guardians of limbo derived their authority from being there, their legitimation as the lone legitimate heirs.

From here (emerging from this tomb), a specific state mourning policy will appear that will consolidate and transform different cultural and political traditions of mourning. A mourning policy that stipulates who must be and who cannot be mourned. A memory policy that scratches out memories like names from books or faces in pictures. A mourning policy that can grant a life after death, just as it can take a life before death. It concludes with Stalin's bombastic 1953 burial and peaks early in the funeral services for Kirov in 1934, flanked by torches and fans, red velvet curtains and palm fronds. With a dramatic kiss on the forehead of his former comrade, Stalin will bring all those present, without exception, to tears, and in the ensuing silence, will whisper into the dead man's ear: "Farewell, dear friend, we will avenge your death"—then the Terror begins (Montefiore, 177f.). Through the enlistment of mourning, through the governance of mourning, under the leadership of a "mourning specialist," the Stalinian state is constructed (ibid., 180). A state of mourning.

A further episode should have driven home the practices of Soviet Power: the protocols concerning the order of invited guests at funeral ceremonies for heads of state. From the time of Lenin's embalmment, the ordering of the guests, who was present and who was absent, gave a sense of who would wind up in a choice position on their climb to power. According to the protocol drafted by the Politburo on January 27, 1924, Stalin and Zinoviev were first and foremost those assigned to carry the coffin from the portico where Lenin lay exposed to Red Square. Significantly, Trotsky was staying on the Black Sea at the time recovering from a mysterious ailment. (Zbarsky and Hutchinson, 6)

Three years later, Trotsky will be liquidated—just exile at first—in the same way that three years before, he himself had carried out a peerless liquidation—not just exile. The liquidation of Kronstadt, of the "pride and joy of the Russian Revolution," as Trotsky himself had referred to the sailors and workers of Kronstadt in 1917 (Volin, 10). The Bolsheviks do not negotiate, do not consider a single one of the communist council's demands. Zinoviev's response to the Kronstadt rebels' invitation to talks is an ultimatum—"Give up, or we'll shoot you one by one like partridges" (Gietinger, 14). And like partridges, sixteen thousand citizens of Kronstadt are shot, by an army with vast numerical superiority, carefully chosen and brought from far away by train, from Ukraine, from Poland, from Lithuania, from China. These soldiers do not defect to the revolutionaries like the members of the first two attack groups, do not react to the citizens of Kronstadt's repeated shouting that they do not want to shoot comrades. These soldiers are not comrades, they do not speak the language of proletarian solidarity, for the most part, they don't even speak Russian (ibid., 22).

Disciplined Bolsheviks, Chekists and commissars, command and accompany the army that vanquishes the Kronstadt Soviet on March 18, 1921, on the ice bordering Petrograd. In hindsight, the list of prominent participants reads like an index of a deferred suicide commando. From the rabble-rouser Zinoviev (shot in 1936) to commanders Tukhachevsky (shot in 1937) and Trotsky (murdered in 1940), all the way down to the opposition politicians who come directly from the Tenth Party Congress to lend a hand: Pyatakov (shot in 1937), Zatonsky (disappeared in 1938), Bubnov (liquidated in 1940). "Kronstad caught up with all of them" (ibid., 26).

Before then, the democratic centrist Bubnov will receive the Order of the Red Banner for the massacre of the Kronstadt rebels, and Alexandra Kollontai from the workers' opposition, the only member of this branch of the opposition not to die at the hands of her comrades who toed the party line, will boast at the Tenth Party Congress in 1921: "We belong to the first volunteers to fight against the rebels" (ibid., 21). At the very same congress of the Russian Communist Party that decides on the New Economic Policy, that opts for freedom of commerce, that chooses to grant concessions to capitalists rather than permit free Soviet elections. At the same Tenth Congress of the Russian Communist Party where Lenin will propose a ban on interparty factions: "The Party Congress must arrive at this conclusion, that the opposition is done for, that it must be gotten rid of once and for all, that we are now tired of the opposition" (ibid., 25).

The demands of the reformist opposition are not unlike those of the Kronstadt revolutionaries. Both criticize the authoritarian leadership and the Taylorist labor regime in the factories; the former favors more self-management for workers over the centralization of the economy, more democracy over the party hierarchy; the latter suggests dispensing with party control altogether. But the Kronstadt critique, articulated in fourteen issues of *Izvestia* down to the last day of the revolution, is far sharper, far clearer, because it bows down to no reasons of state and obeys only the promise of revolution:

The Communist Party, which has studied closely the mood among the masses, wrote tempting solutions on its flags that excited and swept away the masses, promising to lead them into the glimmering kingdom of Socialism, which only the Bolsheviks were capable of building. Naturally the workers and peasants were gripped with overwhelming joy. They thought that finally the years of slavery under the yoke of the landholders and capitalists belonged to the past. (*Kronstadt Izvestia* 14, quoted in Volin, 107)

But the next four years suffice to transform anticipation into bitter disappointment. Under the command of the state unions and the centralist bureaucracy, not only work, but life as a whole became "deadly dull, joyless, bureaucratic, a life lived according to the plans of those in power" (*Kronstadt Izvestia* 14, quoted in Volin, 107). Deadly dull or just deadly, because "instead of freedom for the workers," the communist dictatorship brought "constant fear of the torture chambers of the Cheka," which inevitably responded to protest with "mass shootings and a bloodlust not at all inferior to that of the Czarist generals." It has become clear to the revolutionaries that the Communist Party "is not what it claims to be: the defender of the working class. The interests of the working people are foreign to it. It has taken power and now is afraid of only one thing: losing it" (*Kronstadt Izvestia* 5, quoted in Volin, 93). To the Leninist maxim that communism is Soviet power plus electricity, the Kronstadt Soviet can only respond dryly: "Bolshevist Communism is the absolutism of the Commissars plus shootings" (Volin, 108).

This is the origin of the Kronstadt rebels' main demand—"All power to the Soviets and none to the parties"—with which they renew the promise of revolution. Never, since October 1917, has the revolution been so true to itself, never again will the Soviet Union come as close to the goal of a union of Soviets, a communism of councils, as in these three short weeks of March 1921. Just as in 1917, a euphoric, solidary mood grips the people, and they gather in tens of thousands in Anchor Square in Kronstadt's center, refuse to accept higher wages than their comrades, retake the committees and occupy them themselves. They refuse all support from organized parties, especially those of the Right, the counterrevolutionaries; what they want, as a Petrograd flyer reads, is not "to live by the rules of the Bolsheviks," no, "they want to decide their own fate." It is the "dawn of the Third Revolution" that they declare, the dream of "a different kind of Socialism" that they have begun to make reality (*Kronstadt Izvestia* 14, quoted in Gietinger, 22). Against the "dictatorship of the Communist Party with its Cheka and its state capitalism," they want "to make the unions and the farmers' organizations ... into voluntary association of workers, farmers, and intellectuals (*Kronstadt Izvestia* 5, quoted in Volin, 93).

And perhaps the Kronstadt rebels, the workers, the soldiers would have been particularly suited to carrying a third revolution after the bourgeois revolution of February 1917 and the socialist revolution in October. They came from farm country, they visited on holidays, its misery moved them to rise up, and so they had experience of that class of people that represented 80 percent of the population of this country of 170 million, while the 500,000 active members of the Bolshevik Party had nothing to spare for them but contempt and bullets. The War Communism waged in summer 1918 solves the hunger problem in the cities through forced requisitions carried out by the military, shifting hunger to the villages. This communist war can only be won with brutal armed violence. "In return for the bread, almost all of which was requisitioned, and for the cows and horses that were stolen, they were subjected to raids and shootings. A charming example of barter in the worker's state: bread for lead and bayonettes" (*Kronstadt Izvestia* 14, quoted in Volin, 107). The Kronstadt rebels question the success and the need of this policy. "The peasants," they write, basing their opinion on the experience that the peasants wanted to enter into direct negotiations with the workers, "don't need a commissar to tell them the city needs bread, and the workers can ensure on their own that the peasants get the things they need for their work" (*Kronstadt Izvestia* 11, quoted in Volin, 82).

But that is not the Bolsheviks' approach, and probably not their experience. They see the peasants as a class of small landholders. A class of private owners, kulaks with limited perspectives, who can only be made to see the overriding necessity of social reproduction through violence. "The peasants," writes Karl Radek, looking back, "had just received the land from the state, they had just returned home from the front, they had kept their guns, and their attitude to the state could be summed up as 'Who needs it?' They couldn't have cared less about it" (Werth, 66).

And so the Bolsheviks must educate the peasants in the usefulness of the state. Which is, as Lenin teaches in *State and Revolution*, repression. The Bolsheviks have very quickly become experts in the subject. At Lenin's orders, every peasant found holding a weapon is shot, every uprising is—employing the Bolshevik idiom, rigid from the very first—"mercilessly," "ruthlessly" suppressed—among other things, with poison gas (ibid., 109). It doesn't matter whether they are opposing forced requisition or conscription. Lenin, the Communist, devises a special tactic against the struggles of objectors, of deserters, that is to say: "After the expiration of the seven-day deadline for deserters to turn themselves in, punishments must be increased for these incorrigible traitors to the cause of the people. Families and anyone found to be assisting them in any way whatsoever are to be considered as hostages and treated accordingly"—and this means shot, one by one, until the deserters give up (ibid., 93).

This tactic, today, seems disturbingly familiar, and apparently the Bolsheviks adopted it from the Germans, who took massive numbers of hostages in the 1914 war against Belgium (Gietinger, 1). Learn from the Germans! This motto had a decisive impact on Lenin's politics, including in the economic sphere:

As long as the birth of the Revolution in Germany is deferred, we have the duty to learn from German state capitalism, to adopt it with all our strength, to disdain no dictatorial methods that will accelerate this adoption ... without shying away from using barbaric methods of war against barbarism. [ibid., 1]

It will not be long before his demand is implemented. In *Work, Discipline, and Order Will Rescue the Socialist*

Soviet Republic, Trotsky orders the militarization of the workforce, the transformation of factories into barracks: this will be taken to further extremes during the New Economic Policy, with food rations pegged to individual productivity, working hours extended, and work stoppages redefined as desertion. The protests of the workers who go on strike, the Bolshevik slogan of worker control still ringing in their ears—they do so in 77 percent of the midsize and large industrial enterprises in the first half of 1920 alone—are met by the Socialist state with lockouts and tightened discipline in the factories. Tardiness, absences, strikes are met with draconian punishments—the revocation of ration cards, imprisonment, execution.

The accusations that precede these penalties are "counterrevolutionary behavior," "freeloading or parasitism," "sabotage." Such juridical categories, marshaled to help explain and combat nearly every economic malady, do not individualize, as in bourgeois law, but instead constitute pernicious social groups. As far as possible from economism in any form, what reigns in the Soviet Union is *politicism*, a *policism*, a politics that attributes all social unrest to malevolence and conspiracy that only violence can remedy.

Through the violence of primitive capitalization, the entire society is modeled on the image of a Fordist factory in which all members must act as screws and gears in the service of increased production, and the factory it-self is modeled on the armed forces. Trotsky legitimizes this antisocialist politics with a classic—indeed, *the* classic—anticommunist argument. At the Ninth Party Congress he announces man is naturally inclined to lazi-ness. But while in capitalism, the market compels man to work under threat of hunger, in socialism, it is the state that must do so, inculcating discipline and obedi-ence in workers like soldiers.

Sunday shifts, piecework, extended work hours, lock-outs! There must be a misunderstanding. The people who pursue such policies can only call themselves so-cialists in error, only a case of mistaken identity can lead to these people who justify their policies on the basis of human laziness calling themselves commu-nists. It must be, can only be, a misunderstanding. If only things were so simple. But they are not so simple. Michel Foucault writes in defense of the anticommunist New Philosophers:

Now, an entire Left has sought to explain the gulag, if not, like wars, by a theory of history, at least by the history of theory. Massacres, yes, yes; but it was a terrible error. Reread there-fore Marx and Lenin, compare with Stalin, and you will well see where the latter went wrong. So many deaths, it is clear, could only come from a misreading. One could have predicted it: the Stalinism-error was one of the principal causes of this return to Marxism-truth that we witnessed in the 1960s. Against Stalin, do not listen to the victims; they would only have their torments to relate. Reread the theoreticians; they will tell you the verity of truth. (Foucault, quoted in Zamora and Behrent)

But there is no turning back, no pristine recourse to an innocent, unblemished urtext. The Marxist Stalin—sad as it is—has forever transformed the non-Marxist Marx. When we detach Stalin's head from Marx's cheek—for many volumes now, philological Marxists have been working on separating him from Engels—this complex amputation will leave behind a wound that will never heal. No skin will grow there, no hair. A depilated Karl Heinrich Marx (d. 1883), half his face beardless: henceforward, that is the only portrait of the founder of scientific Marxism that should ever be allowed to hang.

Back to Marx! This movement is intertwined in two ways with the history of Marxism, of Marxist-Leninism, of Stalinism. It is a form of immanent critique challenging the State Socialist leadership for the interpretative prerogative over the concept of communism itself, one that refuses its legitimation through Marxism and in this way constitutes, at the same time, a form of pure critique aimed at the reattainment of an innocence whose sphere of responsibilities and reflective relationship to itself free it from the imperative of a confrontation with the victims of communism. It is thus comparable to another movement that takes place at the same time, one not seldom conceived in opposition to the foregoing, which views itself as an attempt to clarify the question of why, despite the objective conditions of the development of the productive forces that make a communist society possible, capitalism continues to reproduce itself. The answer—the autonomy of the ideological—is conceived of explicitly as a critique of the teleological and economistic determinism embedded in Eastern or traditional Marxism, and simultaneously functions as a deferment, obscuring the uncomfortable question of whether the masses' disinclination to revolution might have historical rather than ideological grounds (cf. Herfurth). As if skepticism toward all the promises of communism—after the revolutions of the twentieth century!—were simply a question of false consciousness and not much more of true.

Communists react defensively to the (anticommunist) critique of communism—not everything about communism was bad—with parries—that wasn't even communism—or by attacking—criticism of the crimes of communism only serves to legitimate the crimes of its enemies. They are right on all counts. But what does it say about communism to state that National Socialism was worse, that capitalism has been just as bad? What kind of verdict is it for communism to say not everything but instead only *almost* everything was bad? Moreover, what claims can one raise on behalf of a communism that despite a century's attempts to realize, only ever

existed as real in the imagination of those who, whenever asked, sadly have no power at their disposal.

Giving up the politics of inverted commas, not attempting to
evade the problem by putting inverted commas, whether damn-
ing or ironic, around Soviet socialism in order to protect the good,
true socialism—with no inverted commas. ... Actually the only socialism which deserves these scornful scare-quotes is the one
which leads the dreamy life of ideality in our heads. (Foucault, 136)

In truth, for materialists, no words are less true than
these: "It was a good idea in theory, but ..." No idea can
be cut off and cleansed from the history of its existence
and take refuge in this state of purity. There is no lumi-
nous socialism untouched by the contingent contamina-
tion of Stalinism. Good theory can no more be cordoned
off from bad praxis than a mere improvement in theory,
a correction of earlier failures, can lead to good praxis.
More democracy, less exclusion, a core of Marx's urtext.
In their abstractness, these attempts seem bent on keep-
ing the concrete historical experiences motivating them
separate from a cherished political-organizational body,
a body of texts handed down to them. One look at the
critique of the state that Lenin formulated in *State and
Critique* on the eve of the revolution, and at the statist
policies he pursued the morning after, is enough to ne-
gate roundly any assertion of a simple causal relationship between theory and practice. Only in appearance,

then, can repeatability be attributed to theory transmissible across history (ontology, representational logic, fetish of work and state) or unrepeatability be used to characterize historical conditions bound by eras (the aggression of the entente, the civil war, the need for accelerated modernization). No, repeatability and unrepeatability are paradoxically interwoven with theory and history. The fact that theory can never be articulated in an ideal space, that both its pedigree and its effects are contaminated by the specific historical constellation, means there remains the danger of a recrudescent failure that mere correction of theoretical errors cannot ward off.

As to the question of insurance against revolutionary risk, the cheap promise—next time it will be more democratic—is offered just as quickly as the only apparently more radical assertion that nothing can, nothing ought to be said about communism's prospects. The prohibition of images, which proscribes the possibility of repeating the present in dreams, turns into a lie concealing the possibility of the repetition of the past in trauma. The dictum that the beautiful image of true communism cannot be shown legitimizes closing one's eyes before the ugly images of false communism. As if it were the responsibility of a certain future, an uncertain future and not of the communists themselves to say why the communism of the future will not resemble the communism of the past. To say why not only another world but precisely a different world is possible. To answer this hardest, most pressing of questions for the communists—who are more than mere anticapitalists, more than critics of capitalist dominance and of every other form of dominance as well—which communists (like the one writing now) have not been able to answer. And the communists will remain unable to answer it as long as they fail to confront the historical reality of communism, its actual movement (cf. Kagarlitski, 14). As long as they fail to focus on the unchosen conditions under which communist choices are made, under which communist decisions must be made.

The material moment of decision when, all at once, the past crashes into the future. The instant of experience into the instant of anticipation. In revolution, whether the Russian or—a cautious generalization—any other, counterrevolution stands on both sides.

The Civil War wasn't desired, but foreseen. That is more than just a nuance. All revolutions since the French one have driven home the following painful lessons: emancipatory movements collide with conservative reaction; counterrevolution follows revolution like its shadow—in 1792, when the Prince of Brunswick's troops marched on Paris, in 1848 with the June Massacres, in 1871, when the Commune was drowning in blood. Since that time, this rule has known no exception, from Franco's Pronunciamento in 1936 to Suharto's coup in Indonesia in 1965 (with a half million dead) to Pinochet's putsch in 1973 in Chile. (Bensaid, 60; Martelli, 223)

Counterrevolution in the past, counterrevolution in the future, counterrevolution in the Russian Revolution's present. Appearing as a painful lesson from the first, anticipating the painful arrival of the second, it strikes against the third, the thirds, because there are more than one. One counterrevolution follows the next, coming from many sides, in mutual persecution, crisscrossing alliances. Of the imperialist entente, the White monarchists, the Cossack lords, but also of the bourgeoisie, the Social Democrats, the Mensheviks, the right-wing Social Revolutionaries whose protests mix progressive and reactionary demands.

Almost always, when peasants, soldiers, workers rise up against the Bolsheviks with antirepressive, democratic, anarchistic demands, anti-Semitism follows not far behind. Nicolas Werth, one of the authors of the *Black Book of Communism*, a book edited with an anti-Semitic slant by Stéphane Courtois, lists them precisely (Küntzel, 252). Death to the Cheka, to the Bolsheviks, to the Jews—so runs the triad of resistance; its equation is Muscovite = Bolshevik = Jew (Werth, 87, 96, 99, 106). Anti-Semitism is a powerful, popular enemy of revolution long before Stalinism makes use of it, and gathers the most various parties into the concept of Judeo-Bolshevism while caring nothing about the party status of slaughtered Jews (Reed, 82, 87). So powerful it is, so popular, that even during the German war against "Russian subhumans," it motivated many of these same subhumans to collaborate with the Nazis (Werth, 215). Already in 1905, anti-Jewish pogroms, most prominently the Black Hundreds, were mounted as reprisals for attempted revolution; the most famous forgery of international anti-Semitism, *The Protocols of the Elders of Zion*, was commissioned in 1898 as an antimodern, counter-revolutionary weapon (Eisner, 61, 138). The Bolsheviks respond with helpless enlightenment, and fatally misjudging the structure of anti-Semitism, hastened obedience, thus reducing the number of Jewish cadres in the middle ranks of the party. Respond too with harsh repression and shootings—like the peasant revolutionary and anarchist Makhno, who fought against the counterrevolution of both Whites and Reds until the latter finally betrayed and defeated him (Arschinoff, 219). And yet they are unable to prevent the murders of 60,000 to 250,000 Jews in anti-Semitic pogroms between 1917 and 1921 (Herbeck, 143).

The White troops act with untrammeled, merciless brutality at first only distinguishable from that of the Reds by their willingness to massacre not only the officers but in particular the low-ranking soldiers. Counterrevolution spares no sacrifice, for those who will be sacrificed are either (in case of its victory) subordinates or (in case of defeat) irrelevant. This is a consummation of the violence that was already a structural feature of the old society; it feels legitimated by a powerful tradition and at the same time liberated from it. Why be an example for the future, if all that is to be copied is the past? Counterrevolution does not fear for its good reputation, it has nothing to lose but its (already lost) dominance.

What revolution could compete with this counterrevolution? Which revolution would be capable not only of overcoming this vicious dominance but also its predictable and predictably even more vicious return? *One* blow against the old is simply not enough, it must always be killed *twice*. The revolution can only be and remain revolution if it anticipates reaction and begins to react to it even before reaction has made its appearance. The revolution can only be and remain as (permanent) counter-counterrevolution. In the compulsion to decide, the question of whether the civil war was desired or foreseen attenuates *into a nuance*. But does revolution remain revolution as counter-counterrevolution, can it, being unchanged, occur a second time? Or will it transform, contaminated by the impressum of counterrevolution? Can the revolution triumph only by adapting to counterrevolution, transforming into a violence equal or even superior to that of its counterpart? Can the revolution only triumph by overtaking counterrevolution, surpassing its hardness, its speed, before it has even appeared?

Are the Bolsheviks not right in April 1918, then, when they dispense with the nonhierarchical council democracy in the army? Is Felix Dzerzhinsky not right when he looks for determined people for the Cheka "who know there is nothing more effective than a bullet in the head to shut people up" (Werth, 68)? Is the Cheka not right to initiate a campaign of unmasking against the five thousand or more former informants and agents from the Okhrana, the czarist secret service, who are taking up important revolutionary posts undetected (cf. Serge, 113)? Should one not agree with Lenin when he attacks the abolition of the death penalty in the revolutionary period as "an error, an unforgivable weakness, a pacifist delusion" (Werth, 69)? The opera lover Lenin, who swears off the opera because he cannot bear to see something so beautiful while he is doing something so ugly. They want to be free of illusions, the revolutionaries, free of illusions and of sentiments that might hinder their progress toward victory. Sentiments like compassion, illusions like that of a just revolution. "Do not imagine," Dzerzhinsky shouts to the communists, "that I am simply looking for a revolutionary form of justice. We have no use for 'justice' at this hour!" (Werth, 58). And what would be the use of revolutionary justice for them, knowing counterrevolutionary injustice could put an end to it at any time? Did they have, under conditions they had not freely chosen, any other choice beyond the inculcation of "resoluteness and hardness," mercilessness and coldness, for withstanding as revolutionaries what they cannot desire to withstand as communists?

Yes—the Kronstadt rebels say. They imprison barely anyone, carry out not a single execution, engage in no revenge. Instead of aggression, they seek dialogue (as long as they still have time to do so), instead of seizing strategically valuable strongholds, they stress that "a true communist should never impose his ideas on anyone" (*Kronstadt Izvestia* 4, quoted in Volin, 78). They trust in the moral force of the revolution and the persuasive power of their arguments, the message of which they broadcast over the radio.

But while the Kronstadt rebels print every single Bolshevik flyer, no matter how slanderous its contents, in their own newspaper, the Bolshevik media suppress all reporting on Kronstadt and instead quite intentionally disseminate the lie that it is a revolution headed by White saboteurs, German spies. The communist leadership reacts to the imprisonment of two communist commissars by taking the families of the Kronstadt rebels hostage. It greets the delegates to the negotiations, who come protected by the parliamentary flag, with bullets—a method it might well have learned from the White officers (Reed, 258). And with the promise of a general amnesty, it lures the besieged, even, years later, those who fled to Finland, back to Russia, only to make them disappear without hesitation to the forced labor camps.

What can we learn from this bloodbath, if there is something to be learned, to apply to a Kronstadt in the future? (Certainly not that in history, the goals achieved overshadow the means employed to achieve them, as Trotsky, at least, might have learned in the end when "his head was caved in with an ice axe, of all things, in the heat of Mexico" [Gietinger, 26]). Would a Kronstadt of the future not have first of all to learn, would it not need first of all to pose the question of why the Kronstadt of the past, despite knowing who the Bolsheviks were, had let them take it by surprise? Would the Kronstadt rebels of the future not need to learn that what they consider impossible is possible, and that what ought not be possible is possible too? Would they not need to recognize the different facets of counterrevolution, the White as well as the Red? And recognizing them, would they not have to anticipate them, and renounce shows of mercy toward them, knowing that these will show no mercy toward them? Should the leftist Social Revolutionary Alexandrov, who opposed Dzerzhinsky's liquidation during an uprising in 1918, not have decided otherwise, knowing Dzerzhinsky would later thank him with a bullet in the head (Gietinger, 8)? Would the Kronstadt rebels of the future not have to take up arms against the Leninists of the future, look on them with suspicion, turn down their offers of negotiations, go on the offensive, and liquidate the Leninists before the Leninists liquidated them? Must the Kronstadt rebels of the future then become Leninists?

But those who must become Leninists to defend themselves against Leninism—would they not have to turn against themselves? Would those who heed the call of violence against violence not be calling for violence against themselves? Because the body, once inured to doing harm (and the joy that doing harm induces in it), cannot simply be taken off like an outdated garment once it is transformed for this purpose.[1] Should they not account for the irreversible transformations that counterrevolution will demand of them? A preliminary precaution, an anticipative institution, insurance against the future? The revolution that accounts for counterrevolution would have to account for its proliferation, for external as well as internal counterrevolution, for this dialectic of revolution. As in a zombie film, the revolutionaries would have to arm their offspring, encouraging them to shoot at them when the transformation process has begun, when the virus of violence sets in. And like the heroes of these films, the revolutionaries to come would have to turn their weapons on their forbears, encouraged by their victims, with tears in their eyes, but certain of the necessity of pulling the trigger. Counter-counter-counterrevolution. It is not its children but its parents that the revolution would have to devour.

The revolution is "per definitionem total, and therefore both extensive and intensive: if it remained local, it would be subversion, if it remained superficial, it would be reform (Loick a, 3). The revolution "is total because it wishes to replace a totality" (ibid., 6f.). Consumed by the apparition of a catharsis through violence, which will return, which down to today will never stop returning, and which draws its plausibility from the immensity of the fossilized massif of tradition, against which it declares war. If it is earnest, it fights against the old, where it is objectified in counterrevolutionary institutions, but also where it institutionalizes itself in revolutionary subjects. It fights and must fight against its own fighters, who are ever in danger of remaining old as they fight for the new. If it is radical, it necessarily turns on itself, because it contaminates itself with the old as it struggles against it. It requires violence to break up what has hardened, to demolish the armor that blocks its path and must be cleared away. That is—and remains—*cleansing*. But to stay in the picture, there is nothing left, no undamaged core that can be salvaged from its shell, no hinterworld that can be blown back open. No beach lies under the shattered paving stones.

Would it not have been better if the revolutionaries had capitulated in advance to the approaching counterrevolution? Should they not have handed over their arms, given up their lives but kept their morals, with no hope of mercy? Wouldn't the communists have been more useful to their later comrades if they had entered history as victims to be mourned? Would it not have been more revolutionary, within the dialectic of counterrevolution, to have let the revolution go?

This is not a rhetorical question, it is a historical one, a real one. A half century after Lenin, Salvador Allende

will have to answer it: the democratically elected socialist administration of Chile, which triumphed without
armed violence, will have to choose whether to order
the socialist majority, the population, to wage armed
resistance against the putsch by the CIA and Pinochet.
The resistance's chances are far from poor, but a civil
war will mean hundreds of thousands dead, decades
of devastation and poverty; nonviolent surrender will
mean decades of dictatorship, the death of the socialist
government and of a few thousand comrades. The government must decide quickly, and quickly it decides—
against itself. Decides for the soccer stadium where,
without resistance, the arrestees are led one after the
other to the wall. They can win the civil war, they know,
but that socialism cannot triumph afterward.

If the alternative appears this way in light of history,
it does so as an aporia. As a contradiction between two
propositions, both equally true, as an irresolvable contradiction. Twofold failure of the revolution, to which
resignation could merely add a third. But the aporia
is not in itself an answer to the problem, as a certain
philosophy would like to have it; it is rather a problem
that itself demands an answer. Everything rises up, everything must rise up against this aporia, which seems
determined to push for renunciation; since historical in-
escapability takes on the logical form of this aporia. But
in the terrain of history, no laws' validity extends beyond
today. There must be historical, manmade conditions

under which it is possible to resolve the riddle of the revolution. But the solution of the riddle is itself a condition, one condition, at least, for the success of the revolution—the coming revolution.

In the brief year of 1917, a series of attempted revolutions rains down like birds in the sky. Two of them are successful, the second in October, the first in February: "We could hardly believe in it, we had waited for so long, but there it was, at last, the revolution," Victor Serge (64) writes in Barcelona. "The improbable became reality. We read the telegrams from Russia and felt transformed." The revolution appears—at last. But not so much on the stage, before the eyes of the zealous public, not so much in the party struggles over parliament, the central strongholds, the capital. Unplanned, without military orders, without legal legitimation, *wildly*, in other words, peasants carry out land appropriations throughout the country, sailors desert or depose their officers. Students write their professors a new history curriculum, soldiers invite their field chaplains to their gatherings in order to "give their lives a new meaning." Hotel staff refuse to take tips, and little schoolchildren demand boxing lessons so their older peers will hear them out and respect them (Bensaid, 59). In the meetings taking place all over, all attempts to limit speaking time meet with resistance, while appeals for less smoking are supported by everyone and obeyed by no one. And the statue of Catherine the Great suddenly brandishes a little red flag

(Reed, 51f.). That is why the Russian Revolution has no anniversary, because it didn't occur in a day, not even in ten. Which is not to say that it may not come to an end after one day, even as it remains unfinished. Solemnly, on October 26, the Communist Party will hand over power to the council, which it had conquered militarily for this purpose the same day. A formal present of Bolshevik mercy. The beginning of Soviet power will be at the same time the beginning of its end. A Soviet Union without soviets, without union. No councils, no unification, only unity. And an ashy sun, which will begin ceaselessly to rise. Or not. Morning of the revolution.

7 PS

To learn to read. In the place where I spent most of the years of my life, on a tiled garden wall that ran along my walk to school, there was a bit of graffiti, a motto drawn out in white streaks, reading simply: "WE ARE HERE." The *A* was circled, nothing else indicated who this *we* might be. I didn't need to know more than that. The narrow handwriting was enough to give me a feeling of security, sometimes even of strength. This *A* opposed fear, but above all the loneliness of a small German city in the nineties.

Acknowledgments

For their collective editing, the author would like to thank Alex Karschnia, Christel Adamczak, Daniel Loick, Dascha Klingenberg, Flo Maak, Greta Wagner, Guido Kirsten, Jakob Müller, Jeronimo Voss, Katja Diefenbach, Martin Saar, Nadine Teuber, Nicola Nord, Ole Schmitt, Rahel Jaeggi, Stephan Wirtz, Thomas Adamczak, Jacob Blumenfeld, Zacharias Wackwitz, Cindy Milstein, and Ginny Crossman.

Notes

Chapter 1

1. In addition, there were an unknown number of "informal" deportations. Just as in Poland in 1939, the new border region where, in the guise of resettlement, ten thousand Jewish refugees were deported, not only by the Germans into Russian territory, but by Russian troops back into German territory. When the SS inquired about why the Russian plenipotentiary Yegnarov did not wish to accept the Jews, given that anti-Semitism was allegedly nonexistent in the USSR, he replied that the Nazis "would soon find other ways to dispose of the Jews" (Schafranek, 61 ff. This book contains 305 capsule biographies of deported antifascists).

2. "At the beginning of 1936 only 15% of immigrants were of Jewish descent, though the proportion was 70% among the refugees from National Socialist Germany as a whole. The explanation lies in the fact that 'racist' persecution was of secondary importance as regards applications for asylum. What mattered was active participation in the anti-fascist resistance" (Steinberger and Broggini, 27). Often even that didn't suffice. The criteria for "political-moral quality" were such that many resistance fighters came to be seen as "unworthy elements" on the basis of their "undisciplined behavior, unbecoming of the proletariat" (Schafranek, 14).

3. "'Bukharin, too, spoke of organized capitalism. Perhaps National Socialism is a form of organized capitalism that paves the way for socialism. The matter requires unbiased observation. This discussion must be put off for a year.' 'Back in Germany, you won't feel like arguing with me,' I said bitterly" (ibid., 692).

4. "As a brief prelude to taking stock we communists ought first of all to hail documentation and polemical treatises (The Black Book of Communism) instead of defending ourselves apologetically. As scientific communists, it is absolutely incumbent upon us, first of all, to update the Black Book" (Schritkopcher, 1).

Chapter 2

1. "5-1-39. Lovely weather. A magnificent display and demonstration! Portraits of D[imitrov] next to portraits of the members of the Politburo. Among the slogans announced by the tribune is also 'Long live D[imitrov], helmsman of the Comintern.'"

> 6-7-39. ... Beginning driving school. ... Steered the car well. On the curve by the sanatorium the car rammed into a tree. It is damaged in the front and R[osa] Ju[lievna] bumped her leg. ... Thank God ... ! (Dimitroff, 262f.).

2. An example is the conflicts in 1980s' Germany a half century later. The "first generation" of the Red Army Faction, the RAF, has spent more than ten years in prison. Irmgard Möller is the only survivor of the Stammheim Death Night. Outside, for the first time since the post-1977 depression, groups that also criticize the RAF are engaging in protests and militant actions (urban warfare, etc.). Oliver Tolmein: "At that time, I had nothing to do with them, but I was with anti-imperialist groups that sympathized with them, and so any criticism of the RAF and the prisoners was taken rather ungraciously." Möller: "Yeah, we saw the same thing on the inside. And it was a grave error not to say anything about it. For us at the time, the most important thing was not to give our enemies any ammunition. We were afraid if we got mixed up in those confrontations, we'd be playing into their hands. Actually this led us to tie our own hands." The (new generation of) the RAF also engaged in further actions in fierce opposition to US military installations. During an attack on a US Air Force base, the soldier Edward Pimental was shot in order to steal his ID card. Tolmein: "If that represented in your eyes a break with what the RAF was and what it did, then you should have said something in public, regardless of the consequences. There was the danger that something like that could happen again, that the RAF was developing in a direction that struck you as totally wrong." Möller: "We were happy at the time that there was so much criticism of the action from the outside, even from other militant groups. We didn't want to say anything ourselves, because we thought that would give the impression we were stabbing them in the back. That could be seen as a lack of solidarity, and we wanted to avoid that at all costs. From my perspective today, that was a rather crazy consideration, and I would never do things that way again. But at that time, we couldn't see another approach" (Tolmein a, 163, 180).

Comparable logic in incomparable circumstances. For this faction of the Red Army found itself, contrary to its occasional self-perception, in a struggle not with the fascism frequently suspected in the United States and Israel (cf. Tolmein b) but rather with post-Nazi Germany, whose emergency decree/suspension of the separation of powers/evasion of the provision against judicial retroactivity/prohibition of collective bargaining and so on may well have worn a fascistic scowl—but then, a smile doesn't make a cat.

3. "'You communists may yearn for the good,' my father said to me once, 'but you have no mercy for the poor. You have no pity for yourselves and so you believe that everything is permitted. Our Savior had no pity for himself, but he loved humanity. You love no one and no one loves you ...' I answered him: Maybe you're right, Father. But maybe you can't save humanity if you love it too much. The Savior wanted to redeem the world, but he didn't succeed. It's not enough to die for mankind, you must kill for it, Father. It's a curse to be a redeemer, the world is too evil, its redeemer can't be someone good. ... We hate poverty, we are indignant. We hate the poor who wait for pity, who even demand it. We want them to become indignant—same as us. Compassion makes you a Social Democrat. Compassion—we've got no use for that. Can you destroy a world with compassion, can you build a new one with it?" (ibid., 23f.).

Chapter 3

1. Just leaving a propaganda event early sufficed for imprisonment. In his speech held at this event, titled "Death to the Gestapo and the Trosky-Zinoviev Mob," Willi Bredel says, "Under Stalin's leadership the peoples of the Soviet Union, despite all attempts at sabotage by the party's enemies, went from victory to victory, created a socialist economy and all the preconditions of a free, happy life. ... Under Stalin's leadership, 170 million people, a federation of the free, were the first in the history of humanity to march toward a classless socialist society. ... Each new success brings us (the German writers present) joy. The soaring achievements of the Stakhanov workers, the progress of the traffic engineers, the heroic deeds of our sharp Soviet airmen, the firm, persistent peace policy of the Soviet Union, the whole of Soviet life, filled with enthusiasm, captivates us German writers and spurns us on to ever more, ever greater achievements. And that we live under good material conditions, under far better ones than we ever had in Germany, is thanks to the Communist Party and to our leader, our comrade, Stalin (great applause)" (ibid., 12). Without hesitation, without shudders, the German-language writers call comrade Stalin their "great leader," their *großen Führer*, whom "every single son" of the people is ready to protect with his life, along with the party and the homeland—so it is written in the *Deutsche Zentral Zeitung* of August 29, 1936 (ibid., 13).

2. "There were no significant strikes anywhere. 'We will write ... the lower functionaries did not understand.' This became the refrain the Party relied on for years to justify its failures. In this formula, the Politburo encapsulated

'Bolshevik self-criticism.' The line was—always—correct, the tactics of the party were—always—correct, everything was good, magnificent. And yet somehow, we failed to stride from one success to the next? Alas, the 'lower functionaries' did not understand" (Sperber 164).

3. In agreement with Marx—"This man for example is only king because other people behave toward him as subjects. And conversely, they believe themselves to be subjects because he is king"—and with an astonishingly clear perspective on the theory of representations, Stalin explains to his son, "You are no more Stalin than I am. Stalin *is* the Soviet Union. Stalin is the likeness in portraits and in the newspapers—not you, not even I" (Marx and Engels b, 72; Montefiore, 15).

4. "By seizing a state monopoly as sole representative and defender of working-class power, the Bolshevik Party justified itself and became what it already was: the party of the owners of the proletariat, owners who essentially eliminated earlier forms of property" (Debord, 86).

Chapter 4

1. "For what attracted me and overpowered me and sufficed for me as a goal was their rejection of tradition. I had hidden the fatal strife with my father like a disgrace and never lost that anxious sense that just drawing a breath without his permission was somehow shameful. My eccentric friends and I never went so far as to side against my father, it was just that they scorned and ridiculed things like raised collars, mustaches, beer, short haircuts, bourgeois clothing—and that destroyed the old man's image" (Glaser, 38). The astonishing familiarity of these formulations gives some sense of how far-reaching counterrevolution and restoration must have gone to make the experience of 1968 seem not like a continuation or repetition but like a new beginning.

2. "People are forever quoting Talleyrand's remark that language is only there in order to hide the thoughts of the diplomat (or for that matter of any other shrewd and dubious person). But in fact the very opposite is true. Whatever it is that people are determined to hide, be it only from others, or from themselves, even things they carry around unconsciously—language reveals all" (Klemperer, 11).

3. How refreshing, by contrast, is this breezy snub from Susanne Sachse in the film *Raspberry Reich*, directed by Bruce LaBruce: "Boyfriend? I don't have any boyfriend. THE REVOLUTION IS MY BOYFRIEND."

Chapter 5

1. "As a general principle, one is all the more right if one has spent one's life making mistakes, since it is always possible to say, 'I went through that.' That's why the Stalinists are the only ones who can give lessons in anti-Stalinism" (Deleuze and Augst; cf. Schmid, 28).

Chapter 6

1. The victim-perpetrator spiral—so typical of Stalinism—sets in motion very early: "By the beginning of 1919, the Chekas had little or no resistance against this psychological perversion and corruption. I know for a fact that Dzerzhinsky judged them to be 'half-rotten,' and saw no solution to the evil except in shooting the worst Chekists. ... In every prison there were quarters reserved for Chekists, judges, police of all sorts, informants, and executioners. ... The executioners generally ended up being executed themselves. They would begin to drink, run wild, and fire unexpectedly at anyone" (Serge, 94).

Remembrance
(Bibliography)

Adamczak, Bini, a. *Communism for Kids*. Translated by Jacob Blumenfeld and Sophie Lewis. Cambridge, MA: MIT Press, 2017.

Adamczak, Bini, b. "Warum mir das Ausbleiben der Revolution auf den Magen schlägt." *diskus* 2, no. 3 (2003).

Armanski, Gerhard. *Maschinen des Terrors*. Münster, 1993.

Arschinoff, Peter A. *Geschichte der Machno-Bewegung*. Münster, 1998.

Benjamin, Walter. *Illuminations: Essays and Reflections*. Translated by Harry Zohn. New York: Schocken, 2007.

Benjamin, Walter. *Moscow Diary*. Translated by Richard Sieburth. Cambridge, MA: Harvard University Press, 1986.

Bensaid, Daniel. "Verbrecherische Revolution—verbrecherische Idee?" In *"Roter Holocaust?" Kritik des Schwarzbuchs des Kommunismus*, edited by Jens Mecklenburg and Wolfgang Wippermann, 51–73. Hamburg, 1998.

Birkenfeld, Wolfgang. "Stalin als Wirtschaftspartner Hitlers (1939–1941)." *Vierteljahresschrift für Sozial- und Wirtschaftsgeschichte* 53 (1966): 477–510.

Brecht, Bertolt. *Große kommentierte Berliner und Frankfurter Ausgabe*. Vol. 10. Berlin, 2003.

Bruce, La Bruce, dir. *The Rasberry Reich*. 2004.

Buber-Neumann, Margarete. *Als Gefangene bei Hitler und Stalin. Eine Welt im Dunkel*. Munich, 2002.

Bühl, Achim. "Der sowjetische Historikerstreit zum Hitler-Stalin-Pakt." In *Der Hitler-Stalin-Pakt. Die sowjetische Debatte*, edited by Achim Bühl, 7–37. Cologne, 1989.

Churchill, Winston. *The Second World War. Volume I, The Gathering Storm*. London, 1949.

Debord, Guy. *The Society of the Spectacle*. Translated by Ken Knabb. Canberra: Hobgoblin Press, 2002.

Deleuze, Gilles, and Bertrand Augst. "On the New Philosophers and a More General Problem." In "Gilles Deleuze: A Reason to Believe in This World," special issue, *Discourse* 20, no. 3, (Fall 1998): 37–43.

Derrida, Jacques. *Specters of Marx: The State of the Debt, the Work of Mourning, and the New International*. Translated by Peggy Kamuf. New York: Routledge, 1994.

Diefenbach, Katja. "Unbestimmtheit als Figur für die Aktualität des Kommunismus." *diskus* 2 (2005): 29–36.

Dimitroff, Georgi. *Tagebücher 1933–1943*. Berlin, 2000.

Dimitrov, Georgi. *The Diaries of Georgi Dimitrov 1933–1949*. Edited by Ivo Banic, translated by Jane T. Hedges, Timothy D. Sergay, and Irina Faion. New Haven: Yale University Press, 2003.

Eisner, Will. *The Plot: The True Story of the Protocols of the Elders of Zion*. New York: Norton, 2005.

Foucault. Michel. *Power/Knowledge: Selected Interviews and Other Writings*. Translated by Colin Gordon, Leo Marshall, John Mepham, and Kate Soper. New York: Pantheon, 1980.

Gietinger, Klaus. "Die Kommune von Kronstadt." *trend*, February 2002, http://www.trend.infopartisan.net/trd0202/t090202.html.

Glaser, Georg. *Geheimnis und Gewalt*. Frankfurt, 1990.

Goldner, Loren. "Der Kommunismus ist die materielle menschliche Gemeinschaft. Amadeo Bordiga heute." *Wildcat-Zirkular* 46–47 (1999): http://www.wildcat -www.de/zirkular/46/z46loren.htm.

Groys, Boris, and Michael Hagemeister. *Die Neue Menschheit. Biopolitische Utopien in Russland zu Beginn des 20. Jahrhunderts*. Frankfurt, 2005.

Haffner, Sebastian. *Geschichte eines Deutschen. Die Erinnerungen 1914–1933*. Munich, 2002.

Hagemeister, Michael. "Unser Körper muss unser Werk sein. Beherrschung der Natur und Überwindung des Todes in russischen Projekten des frühen 20. Jahrhunderts." In *Die Neue Menschheit. Biopolitische Utopien in Russland zu Beginn des 20. Jahrhunderts*, edited by Boris Groys and Michael Hagermesiter. Frankfurt, 2005.

Herbeck, Ulrich. "Antisemitismus seit Beginn der Sowjetunion?" In *"Roter Holocaust?" Kritik des Schwarzbuchs des Kommunismus*, edited by Jens Mecklenburg and Wolfgang Wippermann, 142–158. Hamburg, 1998.

Herfurth, Hubert. "Zur kommunistischen Utopiekollision: Weiter als abschreckendes Gespenst oder endlich als begehrenswerte Möglichkeit?" *trend*, November 2005, http://www.trend.infopartisan.net/trd1105/HH-utopiekollision.pdf.

Hillgruber, Andreas. *Hitlers Strategie. Politik und Kriegsführung 1940–1941*. Bonn, 1993.

Jung, Franz. *Der Weg nach unten, Aufzeichnungen aus einer großen Zeit*. Hamburg, 2000.

Kagarlitzki, Boris. "Der Plan, der Staat, die Demokratie. Es ist Zeit vom Sozialismus zu reden." *Fantômas* 10 (Winter 2007), https://www.akweb.de/fantomas/fant_s/fant010/12.htm.

Karschnia, Alexander. "Anti-Odysseus." In *Die Lücke im System. Heiner Müller, Philoktet*, edited by Wolfgang Storch and Klaudia Ruschkowski. Berlin, 2005.

Keller, Fritz. "Die Achse Hitler-Stalin." In *Der Hitler Stalin Pakt, Voraussetzungen, Hintergründe, Auswirkungen*, edited by Gerhard Bisovsky, Hans Schafranek, and Robert Streibel, 25–31. Vienna, 1990.

Khrushchev, Nikita. *Memoirs of Nikita Khrushchev, Volume 1: Commissar, 1918–1945*. Translated by George Shriver and Stephen Shenfield. University Park, PA, 2005.

Klemperer, Victor. *Language of the Third Reich*. Translated by Martin Brady. London: Bloomsbury Academic, 2013.

Knaudt, Ulrich. "Offener Brief an Roberto Fineschi." *Mailingliste der Marx-Gesellschaft*, May 16, 2007.

Kremer, Ilja. "Zur politischen Einschätzung des sowjetisch-deutschen Nichtangriffspaktes." In *Der Hitler Stalin Pakt, Voraussetzungen, Hintergründe, Auswirkungen*, edited by Gerhard Bisovsky, Hans Schafranek, and Robert Streibel, 17–25. Vienna, 1990.

Kronstadt Izvestia. Issues 1–14 (March 1921). https://www.marxists.org/history/ussr/events/kronstadt/izvestia/index.htm.

Kuhn, Hermann. *Bruch mit dem Kommunismus. Über autobiographische Schriften von Ex-Kommunisten im geteilten Deutschland*. Münster, 1990.

Küntzel, Matthias. *"Auschwitz vom Sockel stoßen*. Zur Entlastungsfunktion des *Schwarzbuches* im deutschen Diskurs." In *"Roter Holocaust?" Kritik des Schwarzbuchs des Kommunismus*, edited by Jens Mecklenburg and Wolfgang Wippermann, 251–264. Hamburg, 1998.

Leonhard, Susanne. *Gestohlenes Leben*. Frankfurt, 1956.

Leonhard, Wolfgang. *Der Schock des Hitler-Stalin-Paktes. Erinnerungen aus der Sowjetunion, Westeuropa und USA*. Freiburg, 1986.

Loick, Daniel, a. "Let It Be. Towards a Post-Sovereign Concept of Revolution." In *Revolutions: Revisited, Revised, Redesigned*, edited by Anke Bartels and Raj Kohlmorgen. Bern, 2007.

Loick, Daniel, b. "Lost. Sarah Ortmeyers Arbeit *Venedig Paris Casablanca New York Wien—Für Walter Benjamin*." *diskus* 1, no. 7 (2007).

Maak, Flo, and Dascha Klingenberg. "Good Mourning. Über die Bedeutung von Verlust und Trauerarbeit für eine emanzipatorische Politik." *diskus* 2, no. 6 (2006).

Martelli, Roger. "Gedanken über ein heißes Eisen." In *"Roter Holocaust?" Kritik des Schwarzbuchs des Kommunismus*, edited by Jens Mecklenburg and Wolfgang Wippermann, 221–232. Hamburg, 1998.

Marx, Karl, a. *MEW 8: Der achtzehnte Brumaire des Louis Bonaparte*. Berlin, 2009.

Marx, Karl, b. *MEW 23. Das Kapital. Kritik der Politischen Ökonomie*. Volume 1. Berlin, 2013.

Marx, Karl, and Friedrich Engels, a. *MEW 3: Die Deutsche Ideologie*. Berlin, 1990.

Marx, Karl, and Friedrich Engels, b. *MEW 4: Manifest der Kommunistischen Partei*. Berlin, 1990.

Montefiore, Simon Sebag. *Stalin: Am Hof des roten Zaren*. Frankfurt, 2006.

Müller, Heiner. *Mauser*. Berlin, 1991.

Müller, Heiner. *Werke 1: Die Gedichte*. Frankfurt, 1998.

Müller, Reinhard, ed. *Die Säuberung. Moskau 1936. Stenogramm einer geschlossenen Parteiversammlung*. Reinbek bei Hamburg, 1991.

Musil, Robert. *The Man without Qualities*. Translated by Sophie Wilkins and Burton Pike. New York: Pantheon, 1996.

Reed, John. *Ten Days That Shook the World*. New York: Penguin, 1977.

Schafranek, Hand. *Zwischen NKVD und Gestapo. Die Auslieferung deutscher und österreichischer Antifascishten aus der Sovietunion an Nazideutschland*. Frankfurt, 1990.

Schlögel, Karl. "Moskau 1937—Eine Stadt in der Zeiten des großen Terrors." *Lettre International* 76 (Spring 2007): 48–56.

Schmid, Bernhard. "Französische Reaktionen." In *"Roter Holocaust?" Kristin des Schwarzbuchs des Kommunismus*, edited by Jens. Mecklenburg and Wolfgang Wipperman, 25–40. Hamburg, 1998.

Schmitt, Ole. "70 Jahre Hitler-Stalin-Pakt: Eine 'mit Blut besiegelte Freundschaft der Völker.'" *Antifaschistisches Infoblatt* 85 (Winter 2009/10): S.44–45.

Scholmer, Joseph. *Die Toten kehren zurück: Bericht eines Arztes aus Workuta*. Köln-Berlin, 1956.

Schritkopcher, Zwi. "Wider den erschlichenen 'Kommunismus.'" *Kommunistische Streitpunkte—Zirkularblätter* 2 (Winter 1999). http://www.infopartisan.net/archive/streitpunkte/ks0203.html.

Serge, Victor. *Memoirs of a Revolutionary*. Translated by Peter Sedgwick and George Paizis. New York: New York Review Books, 2002.

sinistra. "how to QUEER antldeutsch?" *sinistramagazine* (2003). http://www.copyriot.com/sinistra/magazine/sin03/edit.html.

Sperber, Manès. *Wie eine Träne im Ozean*. Munich, 2003.

Spira, Leopold. *"Stalin weiß schon, was man tun soll!* Ein Zeitzeuge berichtet." In *Der Hitler-Stalin Pakt*, edited by Gerhard Biovksy, Hans Schafranek, and Robert Streibel, 43–47. Vienna, 1990.

Steinberger, Nathan, and Barbara Broggini. *Berlin, Moskau, Kolyma und zurück. Ein biographisches Gespräch über Stalinismus und Antisemitismus*. Berlin, 1996.

Tolmein, Oliver, a. *RAF—das war für uns Befreiung. Ein Gespräch mit Irmgard Möller über bewaffneten Kampf*. Berlin, 1996.

Tolmein, Oliver, b. *Von Deutschen Herbst zum 11. September. Die RAF, der Terrorismus und der Staat*. Hamburg, 2002.

Volin. *Der Aufstand von Kronstadt*. Münster, 1999.

Wehner, Markus. "Blutbad nach Quoten." *Frankfurter Allgemeine Sonntagszeitung* 26, January 7, 2007, 11.

Weiss, Peter. *Die Ästhetik des Widerstands*. Frankfurt, 1977.

Weissberg-Cybulski, a. *Hexensabbat. Die Gedankenpolizei—die große Tschistka. Gekürzte Auflage*. Frankfurt, 1951.

Weissberg-Cybulski, b. *Hexensabbat. Russland im Schmelztiegel der Säuberungen*. Frankfurt, 1951.

Werth, Nicolas. "A State against Its People: Violence, Repression, and Terror in the Soviet Union." In *The Black Book of Communism: Crime, Terror, and Repression*, edited by Stéphanie Courtois, Nicolas Werth, Jean-Louis Panné, Andrzej Paczkowski, Karel Bartošek, and Jean-Louis Margolin, 33–268. Translated by Jonathan Murphy and Mark Kramer. Cambridge, MA: Harvard University Press, 1999.

Wirtz, Stephan. "Arbeiterschaft und Nationalsozialismus." Master's thesis. Frankfurt, 1997.

Zamora, Daniel, and Michael C. Behrent, eds. *Foucault and Neoliberalism*. Cambridge, UK: Polity, 2015.

Zbarsky, Ilya, and Samuel Hutchinson. *Lenin's Embalmers*. London: Harvill, 1998.

Zeidler, Manfred. "Deutsch-sowjetische Wirtschaftsbeziehungen im Zeichen des Hitler-Stalin-Paktes." In *Zwei Wege nach Moskau. Vom Hitler-Stalin-Pakt zum "Unternehmen Barbarossa,"* edited by Bernd Wegner. Munich, 1991.

Žižek, Slavoj. *The Pervert's Guide to Cinema*. Directed by Sophie Fiennes. 2006.